Gloves

SUSETTE PALMER

Gloves

GUILD OF MASTER CRAFTSMAN PUBLICATIONS

To Roni and my Wednesday class without whose encouragement it could never have happened and to my husband for his support.

First published 2009 by
Guild of Master Craftsman Publications Ltd
Castle Place, 166 High Street,
Lewes, East Sussex BN7 1XU

Copyright in the Work GMC Publications Ltd, 2009

ISBN 978 1 86108 668 6

A catalogue record for this book is available from the British Library.

Associate Publisher: Jonathan Bailey
Production Manager: Jim Bulley
Managing Editor: Gerrie Purcell
Editor: Gill Parris
Managing Art Editor: Gilda Pacitti
Designer: Robert Janes
Photography: Laurel Guilfoyle

Set in Gill Sans and Ribbon

Colour origination by GMC Reprographics
Printed and bound by Kyodo Nation Printing Co.

Why we love gloves

GLOVES KEEP OUR HANDS WARM AND COZY and protect them from the wind and the weather. They may be worn as workwear or playwear, and can be practical or protective, sensible or sensuous. There is no end to their versatility.

Women, men, girls and boys, we all need gloves. According to the British Glove Association's website, gloves are descended from the primitive mittens worn by cavemen, so they have a venerable history and it is not surprising that folklore and proverbs recognize their importance: people may be described as 'hand in glove' or have clothes that 'fit like a glove' – the ultimate tailoring accolade! They may start arguments by 'throwing down the gauntlet', or if they are more subtle they may be said to have 'an iron fist in a velvet glove'. Even revolutionaries cite gloves – for example Stalin said: 'You cannot make a revolution with silk gloves'. On a gentler note, I am sure we all remember the three little kittens who lost their mittens – a warning to careless glove owners everywhere!

I had a great deal of fun designing the gloves in this book and I hope you will enjoy making them.

Susette Palmer

Contents

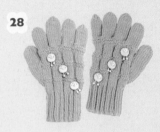

Fun and fabulous. Children will love these brightly coloured
gloves, designed to give them an edge and ensure
they stand out in any crowd.

Child's play

Size

To fit child 8–12 years

Circumference 6¾in (17cm) approx

Measure the actual fingers if possible as children tend to
vary widely in size

Tension

24 sts and 32 rows to 4in (10cm) over st st using
4mm needles

Use larger or smaller needles to achieve correct tension

Materials

Wendy Peter Pan DK Prints 55% nylon 45% acrylic
(170m/186yds per 50g ball)

1 x 50g ball 1320 Tartan

Pairs of 3.5mm (UK-:US4) and 4mm (UK8:US6) needles
if knitted flat, or sets of 3.5mm (UK-:US4) and 4mm
(UK8:US6) double-pointed needles for circular knitting

Stitch holders or waste yarn

Special techniques

MIR and MIL

2 x 2 rib

Pattern notes

Note: In the example, one glove has been knitted on 2 needles and the other glove on 4 needles. Either way works well.

This is a good glove to start with as the yarn is smooth and easy to work, and the variegated colour helps to hide minor errors. You can experiment with knitting on 3 or 4 needles for the fingers. This saves a lot of sewing up and is neater. If you work the first sections on 2 needles you will need to sew up the side seam first to give you 40 sts for the fingers (1 st at each end goes into the seam).

2-needle gloves
(make 2 alike)

With 3.5mm needles cast on 42 stitches.

Rows 1–17: Work in 2 x 2 rib.

Row 18: Rib 21, M1, rib 21. 43 sts.

Change to st st (k 1 row, p 1 row) and 4mm needles. On 3rd row (RS facing) shape thumb gusset thus:

Put a marker though the central stitch (the M1 inc st from the last row). K up to the marker, MIR (see techniques), k the marked st, MIL, k to end.

Work 1 purl row.

Next row: K21, MIR, k3, MIL, k21 to end.

Next row: Purl.

Cont in this way, adding 2 sts on every k row (the M1 on each side of gusset), until the row MIR, k13, MIL is worked – the next k row will be k21, MIR, k5, MIL k21. Cont in st st until work measures 2⅓in (6cm) from rib (RS facing). Place the 21 sts at each end on separate stitch holders with openings towards centre (or on waste yarn) and cont on 15 central sts for thumb. Inc into the first and last st of the next row (17 sts) and cont in st st for 2in (5cm), ending with RS facing.

Shape top

*(k2tog) to end of row.

Purl 1 row *.

Cut off yarn, leaving enough for thumb seam, thread through needle and pull through all top sts starting with the last st on the needle and pull tight. Thread yarn through top sts again for strength. Sew down seam. Leave yarn to neaten up at end.

Rejoin yarn to base of thumb (RS facing) and k for a further 1¼in (3cm) or to desired length, up to base of fingers.

Work fingers

Note: Fingers are worked from the first finger to the little finger.

With RS facing, place the centre 6 sts from the right stitch holder on a 4mm needle pointing right. Cast on 2 sts from the first st. K these cast-on sts, then k the centre 6 sts from this stitch holder and then the centre 6 sts from the other stitch holder, inc 1 in the last st. 15 sts.

Inc 1 st at beg of next row, p to end of row. 16 sts.

There should now be 16 sts for the first finger on the needle and 15 sts on each pin.

Work on the finger sts for 2in (5cm) or to desired length.

Shape top and sew seam as ** (sew the seam as far down as possible to prevent holes between the fingers).

Second finger

Take next 5 sts from RH pin on to needle, inc 2 at front. Knit these 2 sts and the 5 sts on the needle.

Pick up 2 sts from the base of the first finger seam.

Knit the next 5 sts from the LH stitch holder, inc in the last st. 15 sts.

Next row: Inc 1 st, p to end of row. 16 sts.

Work for 2⅓in (6 cm) or to desired length then work from **.

Third (ring) finger

Take 4 sts from the RH pin, inc 2 sts at front, k these and the 4 sts, pick up 2 sts from base of second finger, then the 4 sts from LH holder increasing in last st. 13 sts.

Inc 1 st and purl next row. 14 sts.

Work 2¾in (6.5cm) or desired length and then from **.

Little finger

To keep the outside seam all the way down the glove turn work over and p the 6 rem sts from the holder. Beg at the outside edge k6, pick up 2 sts from the base of third finger, k rem 6 sts from other stitch holder. 14 sts.

Work for 2in (5cm) or desired length. Work from **.

Sew seam from finger all the way down outside edge.

Making up

Tidy up the base of the fingers from the back (see techniques section). *Do not press.* Leave work under a damp cloth overnight.

Smooth out the finished glove and place under a damp paper towel or tea-towel. Cover the damp towel with polythene and place a book or other even weight on top. Leave to dry.

4-needle gloves
(make 2 alike)

Note: This is the same glove, but worked on 4 needles.

Using 3.5mm dpns cast on 40 sts divided evenly between 3 needles and work in the round in 2 x 2 rib (k2, p2) rib for 18 rounds. In the last row (work 20 sts, inc 1, work 20) keeping the rib correct.

Change to 4mm needles and k 2 rows.

Increase for thumb

Mark the 21st st.

Work 20 sts, M1R, k1, M1L, work 20 sts.

Work 1 row.

Work 20 sts, M1R, k3, M1L, work 20 sts to end.

Work 1 round.

Cont as for the last 2 rows, inc 2 gusset sts on every other row until (M1R, k13, M1L).

Cont until work measures 2⅓in (6cm)

from rib. Place sts on thread and set aside.

Cont for another 1¼in (3cm). Break off yarn. Place all sts on waste yarn, tying at the little finger end.

Work fingers

Beg with the little finger, place the last 5 sts from front of waste yarn on a dpn. Place the last 5 sts from back of waste yarn on another dpn. With thumb on right, inc 2 sts in the first of the 5 sts (nearest to thumb). Knit these 2 sts, then the 5 sts on the front needle and the 5 sts on the back needle, to form a circle of 12 sts.

Note: I knit fingers on three needles, lining up the needles containing the sts and working with a third. Pull on the second st of the new needle as you change needles. If you find it easier, use three needles and work with the fourth.

Work for 2in (5cm) or desired length.

Work top

** (k2tog) to end.

K 1 row, pull yarn through all sts **.

Third (ring) finger

Take the next 5 sts from back and front of waste yarn. Inc 2 sts at front as before, k these and the 5 sts from the first needle, pick up 2 sts from the base of the little finger and work as a round. 14 sts.

Work for 2½in (6.5cm) or desired length. Work top from ** to **.

Second finger

As third finger, but place 5 sts from each end of waste yarn on each needle, inc the 2 sts at the front as before, pick up 2 sts from base of third finger, work the other 5 sts. 14 sts. Work for 2⅓in (6cm) or desired length. Then work top **.

Forefinger (first finger)

Place rem 10 sts on 2 dpns as before. Starting from the 2nd finger end, pick up 3 sts from the base of the second finger, knit the 5 sts from the back needle, then the 5 sts from the front. 13 sts. Work 2in (5cm) or desired length.
Then work top **.

Thumb

Pick up the 15 sts left for thumb. Inc 1 at base of thumb. 16 sts. Work even for 2in (5cm). Then work top **.

Making up

Do not press. Leave overnight under a damp cloth.
Smooth out finished glove and place under a damp paper towel or tea-towel. Cover the damp towel with polythene and place a book or similar weight on top. Leave to dry.

Keep your tot's tiny hands toasty warm with these lively mittens. Made in eye-catching pink or stripy blue to make your baby look even more adorable – if that's possible!

Baby's first

Size

To fit child aged 1 year

Circumference 5½in (14cm)

Length 4¾in (12cm) approx

Babies and toddlers differ considerably in size

For a 2–3 year old, make the mittens ¾–1¾in (2–3cm) longer

Tension

24 sts and 32 rows to 4in (10cm) over st st using 4mm needles

Use larger or smaller needles to achieve correct tension

Materials

Girl's mittens Sirdar Tiny Tots DK 90% acrylic 10% cotton (137m/150yds per 50g ball)

1 x 50g ball in 945 Soft Pink

Boy's mittens Sirdar Tiny Tots DK 90% acrylic 10% cotton (137m/150yds per 50g ball)

1 x 50g ball in 0935 Oyster Blue (MC)

Sirdar Click DK 70% acrylic 30% wool (150m/164yds per 50g ball)

1 x 50g ball 0144 Downy (CC)

Both mittens A pair each of 3mm (UK11:US2–3) and 4mm (UK8:US6) knitting needles

Darning needle

To make smaller sizes

Girl's mittens

Cast on 84 sts for frill, then dec as given and work on 28 sts for main part of mitten until work measures approx 3½in (8.75cm). Dec for top and finish as stated in patt.

Boy's mittens

Cast on only 28 sts and work as for patt until piece measures approx 3½in (8.75cm), then dec for top and finish as stated in patt.

Special techniques

3 needle cast-off (see Techniques, page 139)

Pattern notes

Optional buttonhole (to attach mittens to your toddler's coat). Work rows 3–4 of rib section as folls, keeping rib patt correct:

First mitten

Row 3: Rib 9, yo, k2tog, rib to end.
Row 4: Work in rib as set, working yo as a rib st.

Second mitten

Row 3: Rib 27, yo, k2tog, rib to end.
Row 4: Work in rib as set, working yo as a rib st.

Method

Both pairs are worked on 2 straight needles and sewn up at the side at the making up stage. The girl's mittens begin with a frill at the wrist followed by a ribbed cuff and a basketweave-patterned hand, and are then tapered at the top. The boy's mittens are worked in a similar way but minus the frill and the hand is patterned in a two-colour mix of garter and stocking stitch. A buttonhole may be added to each mitten, to attach it to a coat (see pattern notes).

Girl's mittens (make 2)

With 4mm needles cast on 108 sts and knit frill as folls:
Row 1: (WS) Purl.
Row 2: (RS) (k1, k2tog) to end. 72 sts.
Row 3: Purl.
Row 4: Knit.
Row 5: (p2tog) to end. 36 sts.
Change to 3mm needles for rib.
Row 1: K1 (p2, k2) to end, k1.
Row 2: P1, (k2, p2) to end, p1.
Rows 3–7: Cont in rib as set, adding a buttonhole (see notes) if preferred.
Row 8: Work in rib as set, but inc 1 st at each end of row. 38 sts.
Change to 4mm needles and work in patt.

Pattern

Row 1: (RS) (p2, k2) to end.

Row 2: (k2, p2) to end.

Row 3: As row 1.

Rows 4–6: (beg WS) As rows 1–3. These 6 rows set patt.

* Cont until work measures 4in (10cm) approx from beg, with RS facing for next row.

Shape top

Place a marker in the centre of row (19 sts either side of marker).

Next row: (RS) Keeping patt correct, k1, k2tog tbl, work to 2 sts before marker, k2 tog, slip marker across to RH needle, k2tog tbl, work in patt to last 3 sts, k2tog, k1. 34 sts.

Next row: P2, work to 2 sts before marker, p2, slide marker across, p2, work in patt to last 2 sts, p2.

Rep these 2 rows, then row 1 once.

Final row: P1, p2tog, work to 2 sts before marker, p2tog tbl, slip marker across to RH needle, p2 tog, work in patt to last 3 sts, p2tog tbl, p1. Divide rem sts between 2 needles. With RSs of work facing, cast off by the 3-needle method (see techniques).

Making up

Sew side seam. Darn in ends.

Boy's mittens (Make 2)

With 3mm needles cast on 36 sts. Change to MC.

Row 1: K1, (p2, k2) to last st, k1.

Row 2: P1, (k2, p2) to last st, p1.

Rows 3–4: As rows 1–2.

Note: work buttonhole on rows 3–4 of rib preferred (see pattern notes).

Rows 5–6: Using CC, work in rib as set.

Rows 7–9: Using MC, work in rib.

Row 10: Work in rib as set, but inc 1 st at each end of row. 38 sts. Change to 4mm needles and beg patt.

Rows 1–2: Using CC, work in g-st.

Rows 3–4: Using MC, work in st st.

Rows 5–6: Using MC, work in g-st.

Rows 7–8: Using MC, work in st st. These 8 rows form patt. Cont in patt as for girl's mittens from * to end.

Making up

Sew side seam and darn in ends.

Note: Unwind the coloured thread from the given yarn to produce a smooth yarn for sewing up.

Leave under a damp cloth overnight.

These classic gloves, brought up-to-the-minute with a contemporary pattern, are ideal for keeping your hands warm and snug on the coldest of winter days.

Lady in blue

Size

To fit average woman
Circumference above thumb 7⅔in (19.5cm) approx

Tension

22 sts and 28 rows to 4in (10cm) over st st using
4mm needles
Use larger or smaller needles to achieve correct tension

Materials

Stylecraft Special DK 100% acrylic (304m/332yds per 100g ball)
1 x 100g ball in 1019 Cloud Blue (light blue)
1 x 100g ball in 1003 Aster (medium blue)
Sets of 3mm (UK11:US2–3) and 4mm (UK8:US6) double-pointed needles
Waste yarn

Variation

These gloves can be worked without the Fairisle pattern if preferred.

Special techniques

Fairisle patterning

Pattern notes

Patterning begins immediately after the rib:

First stripe sequence

5 rounds in light blue
2 rounds in medium blue
4 rounds in light blue
2 rounds in medium blue
5 rounds in light blue

Fairisle section

Work 7 rounds in Fairisle patt rep foll chart after thumb sts have been set aside on waste yarn at *

Second stripe sequence

5 rounds in light blue
2 rounds in medium blue (finger shapings beg here)
4 rounds in light blue
2 rounds in medium blue

Method

These gloves are knitted from wrist to fingertips in two shades of blue, mixing stripes with a Fairisle pattern. Both gloves are made alike.

Gloves (make 2 alike)

With 3mm dpns cast on 44 sts in medium blue and arrange the sts over 3 needles.

Still using medium blue, work 2 rounds in 2 x 2 rib.

Change to light blue and work a further 20 rounds 2 x 2 rib, inc 1 st at the end of the last round. 45 sts.

Beg patterning on next row (see pattern notes for colour sequence and chart for Fairisle patt).

Change to 4mm needles and work 4 rounds in st st.

Begin thumb shaping

Round 1: K21, M1R (by picking up loop bet sts), k3, M1L, work 21 sts to end.

Round 2 (and foll even rounds): Knit.

Round 3: K21, M1R, k5, M1L, work to end.

Round 5: K21, M1R, k7, M1L, work to end.

Round 7: K21, M1R, k9, M1L, work to end.

Round 9: K21, M1R, k9, M1L, work to end.

Round 11: K21, M1R, k11, M1L, work to end.

Round 13: K21, M1R, k13, M1L, work to end.

Round 14: As row 2.

Place 15 thumb sts on waste yarn for later *. Cont to end of round. 43 sts. Dec 1 st. 42 sts. Place these 42 sts on waste yarn so the ends are at the little finger end, ready to work fingers.

Begin to work Fairisle patt as shown on chart at this point.

Little finger

Place 5 sts from waste yarn at back end on a dpn and, then place the 5 sts from front edge of waste yarn on another dpn.

K the 5 front sts, cast on 2, (this is the bit between the fingers) k the 5 sts from the back. 12 sts.

These are the finger sts, which I find I can work using only 3 dpns, i.e. with the sts on 2 needles and working with the third needle.

Work 2in (5cm) or desired length on these 12 sts, then dec for top.

Note: It is optional (but neater) to use the smaller size needles for the tops of the fingers.

Work 1 round even.

Next round: (k2tog) to end. 4 sts.

Break off yarn and thread through sts to close, leaving a 12in (30cm) tail in case you need to adjust length.

This should leave 32 sts on waste yarn for the rem fingers.

Lady in blue *8 sts x 9 rows*

Each square = 1 st and 1 row
Read RS rows from R to L and WS rows from L to R

■ **Medium blue**

□ **Light blue**

Third (ring) finger

Rejoin yarn. Cast on 2 sts, work 5 sts from first dpn pick up 2 sts from base of previous finger (this forms the bit between your fingers), work 5 sts from second dpn. 14 sts.
Work 2½in (6.5cm) or desired length.
For top, k1, (k2tog) to last 2 sts, k2. 10 sts.
Knit 1 round.
(k2tog) to end. 5 sts.
Break off yarn and thread through sts to close.

Second finger

As third finger but knit 2¾in (7cm) before top.

Forefinger (first finger)

Place rem 6 sts from front and 6 sts from back on dpns. Pick up 2 sts from base of third finger, work 6 sts from first dpn then 6 sts from second dpn. 14 sts.
Work for 2⅓in (6cm) before top.
K1, (k2tog) to last 2 sts, k2. 10 sts.
Knit 1 round.
(k2tog) to end. 5 sts.
Break off yarn and thread through sts to close.

Thumb

Pick up 1 st at base of thumb where it joins hand. Arrange the 15+1 thumb sts on 2 or 3 needles.
Work 2¼in (5.5cm) on these 16 sts.
K1, k2tog to end. 10 sts.
Knit 1 round.
Next round: (k2tog) to end. 5 sts.
Break off yarn and thread through sts to close.

Making up

Sew in ends and leave under a damp cloth overnight.

Your little princess will love these perfect pink mittens edged with a feminine frill. Bright and cheerful, they're certain to bring a smile to young faces.

Pretty in pink

Size

To fit child aged 3–6 years
Circumference above thumb 6¾in (17.5cm)
Length 6in (15cm) approx (adjustable)

Tension

24 sts and 32 rows to 4in (10cm) over st st using 4mm needles
Use larger or smaller needles to achieve correct tension

Materials

Wendy Peter Pan DK Prints 55% nylon 45% acrylic
(170m/186yds per 50g ball)
1 x 50g ball in 993 Tropical Crush
A pair of 4mm (UK8:US6) needles for frill (optional)
Sets of 3.5mm (UK-:US4) and 4mm (UK8:US6)
double-pointed needles
Safety pin or waste yarn

Special techniques

3 needle cast-off

Method

These mittens are worked from wrist to fingertips, beginning with a frill and 1 x 1 rib. The thumb gusset is formed by alternate-round incs, then the thumb sts are set aside on a safety pin or waste yarn while the main mitten is completed. The set-aside sts are then used to finish off the thumb.

Note: To work the mittens without the frill, see variation text on right for alternative starting instructions.

Mittens (make 2 alike)
Frill

With 4mm needles cast on 126 sts.

Row 1: (WS) Purl.

Row 2: (k1, k2tog) to end. 84 sts.

Row 3: Purl.

Row 4: Knit.

Row 5: (k2tog) to end. 42 sts.

Transfer sts to 3.5mm dpns (14 sts on each of 3 needles) and work in the round from this point.

Rounds 1–11: Work even in 1x1 rib.

Round 12: * Rib 20, rib2tog, rib 20. 41 sts.

Mark central st (the 21st stitch).

Change to 4mm dpns and k 2 rounds in st st.

Work thumb gusset

Round 1: K20 (up to marked stitch), M1 (see Techniques, page 145), k the marked stitch, M1, k20.

Round 2: Knit.

Round 3: K20, M1R, k3, M1L, k20. 43 sts.

Round 4: Knit.

Round 5: K20, M1R, k5, M1L, k20. 45 sts.

Round 6: Knit.

Round 7: K20, M1R, k7, M1L, k20. 47 sts.

Round 8: Knit.

Round 9: K20, M1R, k9, M1L, k20. 49 sts.

Round 10: Knit.

Round 11: K20, M1R, k11, M1L, k20. 51 sts.

Round 12: Knit.

Round 13: K20, M1R, k13, M1L, k20. 53 sts.

Rounds 14–15: Knit.

Place the 13 thumb stitches on a safety pin or waste yarn.

Cont on rem 40 sts, pulling tight across the back of the thumb sts.

Work even in rounds until piece measures 3½in (9cm) from end of rib, or approx 5¼in (13.5cm) from start (or desired length).

Shape top

Place marker halfway along round, i.e. between 20th and 21st sts.

Next round: (K2tog tbl, k to 2 sts before marker, k2tog) twice.

Rep this round 4 times more. 20 sts.

Cast off by the 3-needle method, noting that to look strictly symmetrical the second mitten should be cast off in purl. Alternatively, break off yarn and cast off k-wise from the other end.

Thumb

Pick up the 13 sts left for thumb and divide between 2 or 3 dpns. I find I can use just 2 but if you are happier with 3 that is fine.

Inc 1 at base of thumb. 14 sts.

Work even in rounds for a further 1¾in (4.5cm).

Next round: (k2tog) to end. 7 sts.

Next round: Knit.

Break off yarn and pull end through all 7 sts to close.

Variation

To make the mittens without the frill at the wrist, cast on 42 sts on 3.5mm dpns.

Work in 1x1 rib for 15 rows.

Work as for frilly mittens from* (round 12).

Making up

Darn in ends. *Do not press.* Leave under a damp cloth overnight.

Add a touch of sparkle to your outfit, with these gorgeous gloves. Stylish yet practical, these beaded gloves are the perfect accessory for a night on the town.

Beaded diamonds

Size

To fit petite woman

Circumference above thumb 7in (17.5cm)

Finger lengths average as given in pattern (can be adjusted)

Tension

32 sts and 40 rows to 4in (10cm) measured over st st using 3mm needles

Use larger or smaller needles to achieve correct tension

Materials

Cygnet Wool-rich 4 ply 75% wool 25% polyamide (205m/224yds per 50g ball)

1 x 50g ball in 1048 Mauve

Set of 3mm (UK11:US2–3) double-pointed needles

100 small beads (size 8 approx)

Waste yarn

Sewing needle and thread

Special techniques

Bell frill (see Techniques, page 148)

Pattern notes

As hands vary, the bead pattern may be in a slightly different place; it is not placed exactly centrally. If you can, try the glove on (use long dpns, or a circular needle to make this easier), a small adjustment may be made, if necessary.

Method

Thread 50 beads on to the yarn using a sewing needle before beginning to work each glove (see Adding beads, page 150). The knitting begins with a bell frill (optional) at the wrist, followed by 1x1 ribbing. The main part of the glove is then worked, following the chart for the beading pattern and incorporating the thumb gusset. The fingers are then worked individually.

Gloves

Bell frill (optional)

With 3mm needles cast on 155 sts and proceed as given on page 148. You should end up with 56 sts.

Rib

Note: If working the gloves without the frill, cast on 56 sts now.

Rows 1–6: Work in 1x1 rib.
Row 7: Inc 1 st, rib to end. 57 sts.
Work 4 rounds further in st st.

Thumb shaping

Round 1: K28, M1R by picking up a loop bet sts), k1 (st 29), M1L, k28. 59 sts.
Round 2: Work even.
Begin beading patt (foll chart)
Round 3: For right glove, k12, bead 1, work to end. For left glove, work to last 13 sts, bead 1, work to end.
This sets the placement for the beading.
Round 4: Cont beading patt according to chart, k28, M1R, k3, M1L, k28. 61 sts. *
Rounds 5–6: Work even.
Round 7: K28, M1R, k5, M1L, k28. 63 sts.
Rounds 8–9: Work even.
Round 10: K28, M1R, k7, M1L, k28. 65 sts.
Rounds 11–12: Work even.
Round 13: K28, M1R, k9, M1L, k28. 67 sts.
Round 14 (and every foll even round): Work even.
Cont in this way, inc an extra 2 sts every other (odd) row, until you reach:

(k28, M1R, k21, M1L, k28). 80 sts.
Knit one row.
Work up to thumb sts. Place the 23 thumb sts (the M1R, k21, M1L of the last inc row) on waste yarn to work later. Cont to end of row. 56 sts.
Work 16 rows or desired length to base of the fingers.
Break off yarn and work fingers as below.

Fingers

Place all sts on a double thread of waste yarn and tie ends in a bow, leaving 28 sts on each side.
Note: Right-hand fingers are worked palm facing, left-hand fingers with back facing.

Little finger

Place the first 6 sts from the waste yarn on a dpn. Put the last 6 sts on another dpn. Make sure these little finger sts are at the opp side from the thumb with the bead pattern on the back! Using a third needle cast on 2 sts (this is the bit between the third finger and little finger). K6 sts from the first needle then 6 sts from the second. Cont working in the round on these 14 sts to 2¼in (5.5cm) or desired length.
Next round: * (k2tog) to end.
Knit 1 row.
Pull yarn through top of sts and pull tight.
Fasten off *.

Third (ring) finger

Place 6 sts from the front of the yarn on one dpn and 7 sts from the back on another. Cast on 2 sts, k7, pick up 2 sts from the base of the little finger, k7 sts off the second dpn. 18 sts.

Work in rounds for 3¼in (8cm) or desired length. Rep from * to * above.

Second finger

Work as for third finger but to 3in (7.5cm) in length.

Forefinger (first finger)

Rejoin yarn to last 16 sts from waste yarn. Divide between 2 needles. Pick up 3 sts from base of second finger. 19 sts. K for approx 2¾in (7cm) and finish by working from * to * as before.

Thumb

Place 23 thumb sts on 2 needles and work for approx 2½in (5.5cm).

Next round (work top): (k2tog k1) to last 2 sts, k2tog. 15 sts.

Next round: (k2tog) to last st, k1. 8 sts.

Pull yarn through to close.

Making up

Darn in ends and leave under a damp cloth overnight.

Beaded diamonds chart   *17 sts x 37 rows*

Each square = 1 st and 1 row

Read RS rows from R to L and WS rows from L to R

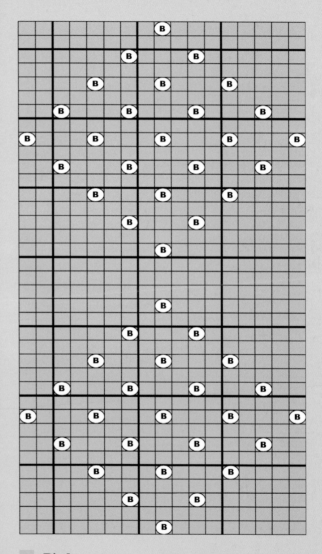

Pink   B = bead

Beautifully designed with intricate details, these fingerless gloves are ideal for all enthusiastic gardeners. Keep your hands warm and your fingers free while completing those odd jobs.

Country garden

Size

To fit average adult
Circumference above thumb 7⅔in (19.5cm)
Length 6⅔in (17cm) approx, adjustable

Tension

32 sts and 36 rows to 4in (10cm) over st st using
3mm needles
Use larger or smaller needles to achieve correct tension

Materials

Jamieson's Shetland Spindrift 4-ply 100% Shetland
wool (105m/115yds per 25g ball) – approx 25g each of
7 different colours
Suggested colours: Violet 600; Plum 585; Sorbet (pink) 570;
Cloud 764 or China Blue 655; Dark Navy 730; Maroon 595;
Leaf 788 or Bottle 820
Set of 3mm (UK11:US2–3) double-pointed needles
Stitch holders or waste yarn

Special techniques

MIR and MIL

2 x 2 rib

Method

For these short-fingered gloves beg at the cuff with two-colour 2 x 2 rib; then commence Fairisle pattern, creating an opening for the thumb with waste yarn. Individual finger openings are worked in 2 x 2 rib with a CC cast-off. The thumb is worked initially in patt to match hand, then 2 x 2 rib and cast off in MC or CC.

Gloves

Rib

Cast on 60 sts in Violet. Divide onto 3 needles and work in the round.

Rounds 1–6: Work in 2-colour rib using Navy for k sts (RS facing) and Violet for p sts, e.g. k2 Navy, p2 Purple, carrying yarn not in use loosely across the back.

Rounds 7–12: Cont in 2 x 2 rib in Navy only.

Rounds 13–18: Resume 2-colour rib (work as rounds 1–6).

Round 19: Cont rib in Violet, inc by (M1, k15) 4 times. 64 sts.

Rounds 20–21: Work in st st in Navy.

Begin chart patt

Work chart in the foll colours:

3 rounds Light Blue pattern on Navy.

1 round Sorbet on Plum background.

3 rounds Light Blue on Navy.

2 rounds Navy only.

1 round Green only.

3 rounds Maroon on Green.

3 rounds Violet on Green.

1 round Royal Blue on Green.

1 round Green on Light Blue.

2 rounds Plum on Light Blue.

1 round Green on Light Blue.

2 rounds Sorbet on Light Blue.

1 round Green on Light Blue.

Divide for thumb

Next round (right hand only)

With Maroon on Light Blue, work 33 sts in patt, work the next 11 sts for thumb and return them to LH needle. Using waste yarn, knit these 11 sts again loosely, patt to end.

Next round (left hand only)

With Maroon on Light Blue, work 20 sts in patt, work the next 11 sts for thumb and return them to LH needle. Using waste yarn, knit these 11 sts again loosely, patt to end.

Both hands: Cont in patt thus:

1 further round Maroon on Light Blue.

1 round Plum on Light Blue.

1 round Light Blue only.

2 rounds Navy only.

3 rounds Light Blue on Navy.

1 round Violet on Sorbet.

3 rounds Light Blue on Navy.

2 rounds Navy only.

Break off yarn.

Divide for fingers

Place all sts on a contrast thread. Tie a bow at the little finger end with 32 sts on each side.

Note: Beg right-hand fingers palm facing and left-hand fingers back facing.

Little finger

Place the first 7 sts on a dpn and the last 7 on another dpn.

Using a third needle, inc 2 (9 sts now on first needle). P the 2 inc sts, (k2, p2, k2, p1) from first needle, (p1, k2, p2, k2) from second needle. There should now be a 16-st circle for little finger.

Note: I usually use only 3 needles but use 4 if you find it easier.

* Work a further 5 rows in 2 x 2 rib. Using Violet, cast off in rib *.

Third (ring) finger

Place 8 sts from one end of the thread on one needle and 8 sts from the other end on another. Cast on 2 sts (10 sts on needle), purl the 2 cast-on sts, (k2, p2) twice on first needle sts. Pick up and k2 from base of previous finger, (p2, k2) twice from second needle. 20 sts.

Cont from * to *.

Second finger

Work as for ring finger.

Forefinger (first finger)

Attach yarn to rem 18 sts with back facing.

From between fingers, pick up and knit 1st, pick up and purl 1 st, then p1 (k2, p2) twice from needle and (k2, p2) twice, k1. 20 sts.

Cont from * to *.

Thumb

Place 11 sts from the top of waste yarn on a dpn and 11 sts from the bottom on another. Using Light Blue pick up 2 sts at each end working in patt to match front on these sts. 26 sts.

Next row: Dec 1 at each end 24 sts.

Work 1 round Maroon on Light Blue.

Work 1 round Plum on Light Blue.

Work 2 rounds Navy.

Now work 6 rounds in 2 x 2 rib.

Cast off using either Navy or Violet.

Making up

Darn in ends and leave under a damp cloth overnight.

Country Garden *16 sts x 36 rows*

Each square = 1 st and 1 row

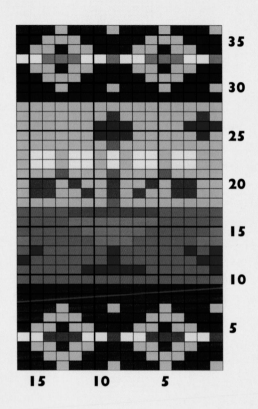

Light blue Plum

Navy Sorbet

Royal blue Maroon

Violet Green

Flip over the top of these simple, yet stylish mittens to transform them into fingerless gloves. Clean and natural looking with a gorgeous floral design, they offer the best of both worlds.

First flip-tops

Size

To fit average adult
Circumference above thumb 8in (20cm)
Note: Because of the 'palm' thumb this may be more comfortable if worked a little wider than usual.

Tension

32 sts and 46 rows to 4in (10cm) measured over st st using 3mm needles
Use larger or smaller needles to achieve correct tension

Materials

Jamieson's Shetland Spindrift 4-ply 100% Shetland wool (105m/115yds per 25g ball) OR or any 4-ply yarn that knits to the right tension
3 x 25g balls in 105 Eesit
Sets of 2.75mm (UK12:US2) and 3mm (UK11:US2–3) double-pointed needles
Oddments of yarn for embroidery

Special techniques

3-needle cast-off method

Method

The mittens start at the wrist with a
2 x 2 rib. The main hand section is then
worked. The thumb opening is created
by working 10 sts in waste yarn then
continuing to work over these again in
the main yarn. Finger openings are edged
individually with 5 rounds of 1 x 1 rib
and loose ends are sewn in at this
point. The flip-top of the mitten is
then worked, followed by lazy daisy
embroidery on the backs of both hands.

Mittens

With 2.75mm needles cast on 60 sts
over 3 needles and work in the round
in 2 x 2 rib for 2in (5cm), inc 4 sts
evenly in the final round as folls: (M1,
k15) 4 times. 64 sts.
Change to 3mm needles and work even
in st st for 2in (5cm) from end of rib.

Begin thumb

K42 (for right mitten) or k32 (for left),
place the last 10 sts back on LH needle
and knit again in waste yarn, knit to end
of round in main yarn. Work in rounds
for a further 1¾in (4.5cm) to the base
of the fingers.
Break off yarn and put all sts on waste
yarn tied in a bow at the opp end to
the first of the 10 thumb sts.

Both mittens

Work fingers (see Techniques, page 144).
Right-hand fingers are worked starting
palm facing, left-hand back facing

Little finger

Place 7 sts from one end of waste
yarn on a dpn and 7 sts from the
other end on another dpn. Inc 2,
work these and the rem 7 sts on first
needle in 1 x 1 rib, then rib 7 sts from
other needle (16 sts) to form circle.
Work 5 rounds 1 x 1 rib.
Cast off loosely in rib,

Third (ring) finger

Place the next 8 sts from each end of
waste yarn on a dpn. Inc 2, then rib these
2 sts and the 8 sts onto one needle, pick
up and rib 2 sts from the base of the
previous finger, rib the 8 sts on the other
needle. 20 sts.
Rib 5 rows and cast off.
Rep above for second finger.

First finger

Place rem 18 sts on 2 dpns. Rib 2 sts
from base of second finger, rib the 9 sts
from one dpn, then the 9 sts from the
second dpn.
Rib 5 rows.
Cast off.

Thumb

Pick up 10 sts from each side of waste
yarn (see Techniques, pages 144–45),
inc 2 sts at each end. 24 sts.
Work for 2in (5cm).

Shape top

Next round: (k2, k2tog) to end.
18 sts.
Knit 1 round.
Next round: (k1, k2tog) to end.
12 sts.
Knit 1 round.
Next round: (k2tog) to end.
Pull yarn through rem 6 sts to close.
*Note: Darn in ends now, as it is easier to
do this before the flip top is knitted.*

Flip top

Cast on 32 sts and work as folls:
Row 1: K1, (p2, k2) to last st, k1.
Work in this rib for 5 more rows.
Now pick up 32 sts along the back of
the mitten 5 rows down. This should
give you a circle of 64 sts around the
finger tops. Rearrange over 3 needles.
Knit on this circle for 2in (5cm).

Shape top

*Note: I found I could do this using only 3
dpns, but continue to use 4 if preferred).*
Next round: (K2tog, k28, k2tog tbl)
twice. 60 sts.
Next round: (K2tog, k26, k2tog tbl)
twice. 56 sts.

Next round: Knit.
Rep these last 2 rounds, knitting 2 sts
fewer bet decs until (k2tog, k20, k2tog
tbl) is worked.
Knit 1 round.
Cast off using the 3-needle method.

Making up

Embroider lazy daisy flowers at random
(see Techniques, page 150).

Darn in all ends and leave under a
damp cloth overnight.

Luxuriously long and sumptuously soft, these long gloves are ideal for wearing on a cold winter's night. They are perfect for keeping your hands and arms warm and snug while leaving your fingers free.

Softly softly

Size

Arm circumference approx 9in (23cm)
Mitten length (from top to tips of fingers) approx
12½in (32cm)
The fabric is stretchy so one size will fit most hands

Tension

20 sts and 22 rows to 4in (10cm) over st st using 5mm
needles
24 sts and 23 rows to 4in (10cm) over 2 x 2 rib (unstretched)
using 5mm needles
Use larger or smaller needles to achieve correct tension

Materials

Sirdar Blur 30% kid mohair 70% microfibre (190m/208yds
per 50g ball)
1 x 50g ball in 715 Cherish
Set of 5mm (UK6:US8) double-pointed needles
Waste yarn and/or stitch holders

Sizing

For a more petite size, use needles one size smaller to work 4 rows in 2 x 2 rib before starting cable patt (but make sure the cast-on edge is not too tight for your arm).

Special techniques
2 x 2 rib
Cabling

Pattern notes
C10F Cable 10 forward (slip next 5 sts to front onto cable needle, k5, then k5 from cable needle)

Method
The forearm is knitted first as a long piece, then the main hand section. At this point there are several options, to complete the project as open-topped mittens, handwarmers or gloves. There is a central cable pattern on the back of the arm/hand, bordered by 2 x 2 rib throughout.

Right glove
Cast on 44 sts and work 2 rows in 2 x 2 rib. Now set cable patt as folls;

Cable pattern
Row 1: P2, k2, p2, C10F, p2, (k2, p2) 6 times, k2. 44 sts.
Rows 2–6: P2, k2, p2, k10, p2, (k2, p2) 6 times, k2.
These 6 rows form the cable patt and are repeated throughout.
Note: Place a marker at the beg of the round and arrange sts so that the cable panel is on a single needle.
Work as set for 9½in (24cm) or desired length.

Set thumb
Work 22 sts, (work the next 8 sts, then return them left needle and k in waste yarn), cont in Blur to end of round. Cont in Blur, keeping patt correct as set in rows 1–6 above until work measures 12in (30cm) or desired length.

Variations
Open-topped mittens: Change to 4.5mm dpns and work rib for 6 rows, ribbing (k2, p2) twice, (k2, p2) across cable sts, (k2, p2) to end. Cast off.
Handwarmers: Work fingers as per instructions as below (I used 5mm needles but if you have slim fingers use 4.5mm needles). Work finger lengths to about ¾in (2cm) or desired length.

Gloves: Cont until fingers are desired length and work tops by working (k2tog) to end for 1 round (for fingers with odd number of sts, end with a k1). Pull yarn through. See Techniques, page 136, for average finger lengths.

Fingers (handwarmers or gloves):
Break off yarn. Beg with palm facing, thumb on right, aiming to keep the rib and cable as correct as possible.

Little finger
Put first 17 sts of round onto waste yarn or stitch holder leaving next 5 sts on dpn for front of little finger and next 5 on another dpn for back of little finger. Put rem sts on a length of waste yarn or stitch holder.
Inc 2 on front needle. Work these sts as (p1, k1), then k1, p2, k2 from front needle, p2, k1, p1 from back needle. 12 sts.
Work as set for 5 rows, then cast off.

Third (ring) finger
Take 5 sts from the front waste yarn and 6 from the back (this should take you to half-way across the cable sts). On front, inc 2 sts working as p2, k2, p2, k1 from front needle, pick up 2 sts from base of little finger working as k1, p1, work (p1, k5) from back needle. 15 sts.
Work as set for 5 rows, then cast off.

Second finger

Take next 6 sts from front and 5 sts from back. On front, inc 2 and work as (p1, k1), then (p2, k2, p2) from front, pick up 2 sts from base of previous finger working as (k1, p1), then k5 from back. 15 sts.

Forefinger (first finger)

Work rem 6 sts from back and 6 from front.

Pick up 2 sts from base of previous finger working (p1, k1), then (k2, p2, k2) from back and (p2, k2, p2) from front. 14 sts.

Return to thumb

Keeping the rib as straight as possible, (k2, p2) twice along the bottom and as near as you can get to this, noting that the sts are upside-down along the top (if they are slightly off this will not be noticeable), withdraw the waste yarn placing 8 sts on 2 dpns from either side of the waste yarn.

Work (k2, p2) twice along the bottom, pick up 2 sts and work as k2, (p2, k2) twice along top sts, pick up 2 sts and work as p2. 20 sts. Cast off.

Left glove

Cast on 44 sts and work rib as for right hand. Now set cable patt as folls:

Cable pattern

Row 1: (K2, p2) three times, C10F, (p2, k2) 5 times, p2. 44 sts.

Rows 2–6: (k2, p2) 3 times, k10, (p2, k2) 5 times, p2.

Rep these 6 rows throughout for patt. Work to thumb.

Note: Work fingers and thumb as for right hand but pick up and work sts as folls:

Thumb

Work the first 14 sts, (work the next 8 sts and replace on left needle, then knit these sts using waste yarn), cont in Blur, keeping patt correct up to fingers.

Little finger

Beg with back facing and thumb on right, pick up 5 sts from back and 5 from front. Inc 2 sts and work as (k1, p1), then (p1, k2, p2) from front, (k2, p2, k1) from back. 12 sts.

Third (ring) finger

Pick up 6 sts from back and 5 sts from front. Inc 2 sts and work as p2, (k5, p1) from front, pick up 2 sts working them as (p1, k1), then (k1, p2, k2) from other needle. 15 sts.

Second finger

Pick up 5 sts from back and 6 sts from front. Inc 2 sts on first needle and work as (k1, p1), k5 sts from back, pick up 2 sts working them as (p1, k1), then (p2, k2, p2) from front. 15 sts.

Forefinger (first finger)

Pick up 6 sts from back and 6 sts from front. Pick up 2 from base of previous finger working (p1, k1), then (k2, p2, k2) from back and (p2, k2, p2) from front. 14 sts.

On all fingers: Work 5 rows as set. Cast off.

Making up

Darn in loose ends and leave under a damp cloth overnight.

One for the boys. Keep your hands warm throughout the cold winter months with these warm, hard-wearing gloves designed in a masculine blue.

Men's cable gloves

Size

To fit average adult male

Circumference above thumb 8in (20cm) approx (cable panel will stretch if necessary)

Finger lengths as given within pattern (can be adjusted)

Tension

30 sts and 40 rows to 4in (10cm) measured over st st using 3.5mm needles

Use larger or smaller needles to achieve correct tension

Materials

Rowan Pure 4 ply 100% superwash wool (160m/174yds per 50g ball)

2 x 50g balls in 410 Indigo

Set of 3.5mm (UK9–10:US4) double-pointed needles

Cable needle

Pattern notes

C4F Cable 4 forward (slip next 2 sts to front onto CN, k2, then k2 from CN)

C8F Cable 8 forward (slip next 4 sts to front onto CN, k4, then k4 from CN)

Method

These gloves are knitted from wrist to fingertips and have a cable pattern on the back of both hands. The left glove is made in a similar way to the right but there are a few differences (see below).

Right glove

Cast on 66 sts and distribute evenly over 3 needles.

Foundation rounds 1–2: K2, p2, k2 (p2, k4, p2, k8, p2, k4, p2) to set cable patt, (k2, p2) 9 times. 66 sts.

Place a marker for the start of the row and one each side of the cable panel. Keeping the 2 × 2 rib as set, work the 24-st cable patt as folls, noting that it is set out in rows for clarity:

Cable pattern

Row 1: (P2, C4F, p2, C8F, p2, C4F, p2).
Row 2: (P2, k4, p2, k8, p2, p4, p2).
Rows 3–4: As row 2.
Row 5: (P2, C4F, p2, k8, p2, C4F, p2).
Rows 6–8: As row 2.
These 8 rows form cable patt.
Work as set for 3in (7.5cm) approx ending on a row 4 of patt.
Next round: (patt row 5) Keeping

the 24 patt sts correct, k rest of round. Place a marker after 36 sts. There should be 36 sts between markers with the cable patt for the back and 30 sts for the front, and 6 sts each side of the cable panel (6+24+6=36).

Note: Keep the cable pattern correct throughout the hand up to the fingers.

Next round: (Patt row 6) Beg thumb gusset (3 sts towards the front) as folls: K39, M1, k27 to end of round.

Round 7: Cont with the pattern panel, knitting the made stitch.

Round 8: Work to 3 sts past second (39 st) marker. M1R, k1, M1L, work to end.

Next 2 rounds: (Rows 1–2 of patt) Work 39, k3 across the (M1R, k1, M1L), k27.

Next round: (Row 3 of patt) Work 39, M1R, k3, M1L, work to end.

Next 2 rounds: Work 39, k5, k27.
Cont in this fashion adding two M1 sts every 3 rounds until the row M1R, k17, M1L has been worked.
Work without inc to 3¼in (8cm) approx from rib (or desired length). This completes the thumb gusset.

Next round: Work 39 sts, place the 19 gusset stitches (M1, k17, M1) on a stitch holder (or waste yarn) for the thumb. Cont to end of round, pulling tight across back of thumb sts. Work for a further 1¼in (3cm) or desired length to base of little finger.
Note: I began the little finger slightly lower than the others, but this is not essential.

Ending with a row 1 of pattern works well but is not critical.

Work the cables and then work to the last 10 sts of the round. K into the front and back of the next st.

Place the last 9 sts of round on a holder (or waste yarn) tog with the first 7 sts of next round. These are the little finger sts.

Cont by knitting into the front and back of the next st, pulling the yarn tight behind the little finger stitches (these 2 inc sts will form the thumb gusset or fourchette between the third and the little finger).

Work 2 or more rounds depending on how much lower the little finger is than other fingers, keeping the pattern correct on these 52 sts.

Work fingers starting with the little finger. Place rem sts on holders or waste yarn with ends facing little finger. With palm facing place the 7 front sts reserved for the little finger on a dpn and the back 9 sts on another dpn. Pick up 1 st from bet the fourchette sts cast on 2 rows previously, k the picked-up st, then the 7 sts of the first dpn and then the 9 sts from the back dpn. 17 sts (for the little finger). Work in the round on these stitches for 2½in (6cm)

Note: All finger lengths are average and can be adjusted as required.

Work top

K2tog to last st, k1. 9 sts.
Knit 1 round.
Next round: (k2tog twice), k1, (k2tog to end. 5 sts.
Pull yarn through all 5 sts and pull then thread it through again for strength. Leave about 12in (30cm) of yarn and break off. Do not finish top of fingers until end in case there are slight length adjustments needed.

Third (ring) finger

With palm facing, take 7 sts from the front and 9 from the back (this should take you to the centre of the cable panel).
Cast on 3 from the first st, k2, k2tog, k6 from the front, pick up 2 sts from base of previous finger, and then 9 sts from the back. Cont on these 20 sts for 3in (7.5cm).
Work top as for little finger, noting that there will be 10 sts after first dec and 5 sts after second dec (k2tog to end).

Second finger

Work 8 sts from front, 9 sts from back. Inc 3 sts as for third finger, k2, k2tog, k7, on front needle, pick up and k2 from base of third finger, k9 sts from back. Work on thses 21 sts for 3⅓in (8.5cm). Now work top as for little finger, noting there will be 11 sts after the first dec and 6 sts after the second dec.

Forefinger (first finger)

Place the last 19 sts on 2 dpns. With back facing pick up 2 sts from the base of second finger, k9. Work on these 21 sts for 3in (7.5cm). Dec as for second finger.

Thumb

Put sts back onto needles starting by picking up and knitting 3 sts at base of thumb. 22 sts. Work for 2¾in (7cm). Dec as for fingers, noting that first dec is (k2tog) to end.

Left glove

Worked much as for right glove, noting differences as folls.
Cast on 66 sts, setting cable as folls: (k2, p2) 9 times (24-st cable bracket), k2, p2, k2. Work to end of rib. Thumb gusset will start as folls: k27, M1, k39.

Fingers

Pick up back facing, except for the last finger which is picked up front facing.

Making up

Darn in all ends and leave under a damp cloth overnight.

Add some glitzy glamour to any outfit with these fabulous full-length gloves. Choose between sparkling silver handwarmers or racy red mittens for effortless chic on any occasion.

Sparkly swirl

Size

To fit most women (fabric is very stretchy)
Length to wrist 9½in (24cm) approx
Wrist to knuckle 3¾in (9.5cm) approx

Tension

This mitten is very stretchy and the length can be adjusted
Approx 18 sts and 45 rounds to 4in (10cm) stretched
using 3mm needles
Use larger or smaller needles to achieve correct tension

Materials

Twilley's Goldfingering 80% Viscose 20%
Metallised Polyester (200m/218yds per 50g ball)
Red mittens (shaped thumb)
2 x 50g balls in 38 Red
A set of 2.75mm (UK12:US2) double-pointed needles
Silver handwarmers (no thumb shaping)
2 x 50g balls in 05 Silver
A pair of 2.75mm (UK12:US2) straight needles
Both pairs
Stitch markers
Thread or safety pin (to use as stitch holder)

Pattern notes

Lace pattern in the round

Rounds 1, 2 and 4: (P4, k5) to end

Round 3: (P4, k2tog, yo, k1, yo, skpo)
to end.

These 4 rounds form the patt and
are repeated.

Method

The red mittens are worked in the
round on double-pointed needles,
with shaping worked for the hand
and thumb. To wear, put on and swirl
round arm in a circular movement.

The silver handwarmers are worked
in rows on 2 needles, with g-st seam
sts (1 st at each edge). The seam is
joined leaving a thumb opening.

Red mittens

Cast on 63 sts divided bet 3 dpns.
Work in lace patt in the round until
piece measures 3½in (9cm), ending on
a round 4 of patt.

Next round: P1, p2tog, p1, k5 to end.
*Note: There will now be 3 purl sts bet the
lace patts.*

Cont on these sts for a further 3in
(7.5cm), ending on a round 4 of patt.

Next round: (P1, skpo, k5) to end
(2 purl sts bet the lace patts).

Cont on these sts for a further 3in
(7.5cm), ending on a round 4 of patt.

Next round (inc for hand): (p1, M1, p1, k5) to end. (3 purl sts bet lace patts).

Cont to work even in patt until work measures 12 in (30.5) from start, ending on a round 4 of patt.

Round 1 (inc for thumb): Keeping patt correct, work 29 sts, place marker, p1, M1, p1, place marker, work to end of round. 32 sts.

Round 2: Work to marker, (p1, k1, p1) bet markers, work to end.

Round 3: Work to marker, (p1, M1, k1, M1, p1) bet markers, work to end.

Note: Incs are on odd-numbered rounds.

Round 4: Work (p1, k3, p1) bet markers.

Round 6: P2, k5, p2.

Round 7: P1, M1R, p1, k2tog, yf, k1, yf, skpo, p1, M1L, p1.

Round 8: P3, k5, p3.

Round 9: P1, M1R, p2, k5, p2, M1L, p1.

Round 10: P4, k5, p4.

Round 11: P1, M1R, p3, lace patt 5, p3, M1L, p1.

Round 12: P5, k5, p5.

Round 13: P1, M1R, p4, k5, p4, M1L, p1.

Round 14: P6, k5, p6.

Round 15: P1, M1R, p5, lace patt 5, p5, M1L, p1.

Round 16: P7, k5, p7.

Round 17: P1, M1R, p6 k5, p6, M1L, p1. 21 sts bet markers.

Round 18: Work to marker, place next 18 sts on a pin or thread, work to end. 63 sts.

Cont until work measures 12in (30.5cm) or required length.

Cast off loosely in rib.

Thumb

Replace thumb sts on needles. Keeping central lace patt correct and working the other sts in purl, inc 2 sts at base of thumb (23 sts) and work for approx ½in (1cm).

Cast off loosely in rib.

Darn in ends.

Silver handwarmers

Using straight needles, cast on 65 sts. Place stitch markers on first and last sts.

Lace pattern 1

Row 1: K1, (p4, k5) to last st, k1.

Rows 2 and 4: K1, (p5, k4) to last st, k1.

Row 3: K1, (p4, k2tog, yo, k1, yo, skpo) to last st, k1.

These 4 rows form lace pattern 1. Rep until work measures 3½ in (9cm), ending on a row 4 of lace patt 1.

Next row (dec for wrist): K1, (p1, p2tog, p1, k5) to last st, k1.

Note: There will now be 3 purl sts bet lace patts.

Lace pattern 2

Row 1: K1, (p3, k5) to last st, k1.

Rows 2 and 4: K1, (p5, k3) to last st, k1.

Row 3: K1, (p3, k2tog, yo, k1, yo, skpo) to last st, k1.

Cont on these sts for a further 3in (7.5cm), ending with row 4 of patt 2. Length should now be 6½in (16.5cm).

Next row (dec): K1, (p1, skpo, k5) to last st, k1. *There will now be 2 purl sts bet lace patts.*

Lace pattern 3

Row 1: K1, (p2, k5) to last st, k1.

Row 2 and 4: K1, (p5, k2) to last st, k1.

Row 3: K1, (p2, k2tog, yo, k1, yo, skpo) to last st, k1.

Cont on these sts for a further 3in (7.5cm), ending with row 4 of patt 3.

Next row (inc for hand): K1, (p1, m1, p1, k5) to last st, k1. *There will now be 3 purl sts bet lace patts.*

Now work in lace patt 2 until work measures 12in (30.5cm) or required length, ending with a round 4 of patt 2. Cast off loosely in rib.

Making up

Sew seam, leaving an opening for thumb. Darn in ends and leave under a damp cloth overnight.

Cheery and bright, these mittens will match your children's rosy red cheeks. Their practical and bold design will suit children of any age or gender.

Northern star

Size

To fit child 4–6(6–8) years (approx)

Circumference 6(6½)in [15(16.5)cm]

Overall length 7(7¼)in [17.5(18.5)cm]

Length from wrist to top 4¾(5)in [12.5(13.5)cm]

Tension

24 sts and 28 rows over patt using 4mm needles

Use larger or smaller needles to achieve correct tension

Materials

Stylecraft Special DK 100% acrylic (295m/322yds per 100g ball)

1 x 100g balls in 1010 Matador

1 x 100g balls in 1011 Midnight

A set each 3.25mm (UK10:US3) and 4mm (UK8:US6) double-pointed needles

Special techniques

Fairisle

3-needle cast-off

Pattern notes

You can easily adjust the length of the mittens to suit your child's hand size

Special abbreviations

MB Make bobbles

(K1, p1, k1) into first st, turn.

Beg with a p row, work 3 rows st st on these 3 sts only.

Next row: K3tog tb.

Method

These mittens are knitted from the wrist upwards, beginning with a 1 x 1 rib followed by a row of little bobbles at the wrist. A second colour is then introduced and a Fairisle pattern is worked. The tops of the mittens are tapered and cast off using the 3-needle method, then the thumb is completed.

Mittens

With 3.25mm needles and Matador cast on 36(40) sts and work in 1x1 rib for 2in (5cm).

Change to 4mm needles and k 2 rows.

Next row: (MB, k3) to end.

K 2 rows.

Begin Fairisle pattern

Join in Midnight and work the first 10 rows of the chart.

Now work the thumb row, noting that each mitten is worked differently.

Thumb round (mitten 1): Work the first 18(20)sts. Work the next 7 sts, return them to the left needle, and work them again using waste yarn. Cont in main yarn only.

Thumb round (mitten 2): Work first 11(13)sts. Work the next 7 sts, return them to the left needle, and work them again using waste yarn.

Both mittens: Cont in main yarn and work until piece measures 6¾(7)in [17(18)cm].

Next round (dec for top): Place marker halfway at 18(20) sts, (k2tog tbl, work to 2 sts before marker, k2tog) twice.

Rep this dec on every round until 10 sts rem in each half. 20 sts.

Cast off using the 3-needle method, making sure the top lies flat.

Note: To be strictly symmetrical, cast one mitten off k-wise and the other p-wise.

Thumb

Pick up 7 sts both above and below the waste yarn, the 'above' 7 sts on one dpn and the 'below' 7 sts on another.

Round 1: Pick up 1 st at base of thumb, k7, pick up 1 st at other side of thumb, k7. 16 sts.

Rounds 2–3: Knit.

Round 4: Dec 1, k6, dec 1, k6. 14 sts.

Work even for 1¼in (3.5cm) or ½in (1cm) less than desired length.

Next round: (k2tog, k1) to last 2 sts, k2tog. 9 sts.

Next round: (k2 tog) to last 3 sts, k3tog. 4 sts.

Break off yarn and pull end through sts to close.

Making up

Darn in all ends and leave under a damp cloth overnight to block.

Dance your heart out with these sophisticated and elegant gloves inspired by fantastic Flamenco dresses. What better way to top off your outfit and feel like the belle of the ball?

Fiesta

Size

To fit teen/petite (average adult)
Circumference 7(7.5)in [17.5cm(19.25)cm]
Wrist to thumb 3½(3¾)in [9(9.5)cm] (you can make this shorter by omitting the last row of spots)

Tension

28 sts and 36 rows to 4in (10cm) over st st using 3.75mm needles
Use larger or smaller needles to achieve correct tension

Materials

Debbie Bliss Rialto 4ply 100% Merino wool
(180m/198yds per 50g ball)
1 x 50g ball in 09 Red
1 x 50g ball in 03 Black
A pair each 2.5mm (UK13:US1) and 3.75mm
(UK9:US5) needles
Stitch holders

Special techniques

Intarsia

Pattern notes

Spots

Row 1 (inc): (k1, yo, k1, yo, k1) into st (as shown on chart). 5 sts.

Rows 2 and 4: Purl.

Row 3: Knit.

Row 5 (dec): Sl2 p-wise, k3tog, p2sso. 1 st.

Break off Red yarn and pull on the ends to round off the spot. When you are happy that it is a good shape, finish it off by using the two ends to tie a double knot (WS). Darn in the ends.

Method

These spotty mittens are knitted on two needles throughout. Spots are worked as intarsia in Red, against a Black st st background. They begin with a frill at the wrist that tapers to a narrow rib, followed by intarsia spots on the main mitten and short finger shapings.

Mittens

Frill

With 3.75mm needles and Red, cast on 150 sts and purl 1 row.

Next row: (WS) Change to Black and purl 1 row.

Cont in Black, work 8 rows in st st.

Dec row: (k1, k2tog) to end. 100 sts.

Work 3 more rows in st st.

Dec row: (p2tog) to end. 50 sts.

Change to 2.5mm needles and work 8 rows in 1 x 1 rib.

Last row of rib

Smaller size: Inc 1 st. 51 sts.

Larger size; Inc 4 sts as folls:
(rib 10, M1) 5 times, rib 10. 55 sts.

Change to 3.75 needles and work 2 rows g-st in Red.

Change to Black and work in patt foll chart. Rep chart after marking off the central 26th(28th) st for gusset. *At the same time* work thumb gusset on row 7 as folls:

Row 7: M1R, k1, M1L.

Alternate/non-inc rows: On RS, knit across gusset; on WS, purl across gusset on WS.

Row 11: M1R, k3, M1L.

Row 13: M1R, k5, M1L.

Cont to inc 2 sts (as set) on every other row until

Row 23: (M1R, k15, M1L).

Work next row and turn, RS facing, ready to work thumb.

Thumb

Row 25: K25(27) sts, inc in next st, work 17 sts, inc in the last st, turn.

Change to 3.75mm needles and work 5 rows in x1 rib on these 19 sts. *

Change to Red and knit 1 row.

Cast off in Red.

Work rest of hand on rem 50(54) sts until piece measures 3½(3¾)in [9(9.5)cm] from wrist.

Forefinger (first finger)

Knit 18, inc in next st, work 14 sts, inc in last st. 16 sts for first finger.

Turn, work in rib * to * as for thumb, inc 1 at each end of next row. 18 sts. Fold glove in half as in wear. Place rem sts on stitch holders (1 st at front, 1 st at back) with thumb to left.

Second finger

Beg at side away from thumb, pick up and knit 6 (7) sts next to first finger, (inc in first st), pick up 2 sts from base of last finger, k6 (inc in last st). 16 (18) sts. Work * to *.

Third (ring) finger

As for second finger, picking up sts from second finger.

Little finger

K6, pick up 2 sts from base of third finger, k6. Finish by working * to *.

Making up

Pin out frill and place under a damp cloth. Put a polythene bag over mitten to prevent colours running. Place a book on top of frill and fingers, avoiding the spots. Leave until dry.

Fiesta chart *27 sts x 35 rows*

Each square = 1 st and 1 row

Read RS rows from R to L and WS rows from L to R

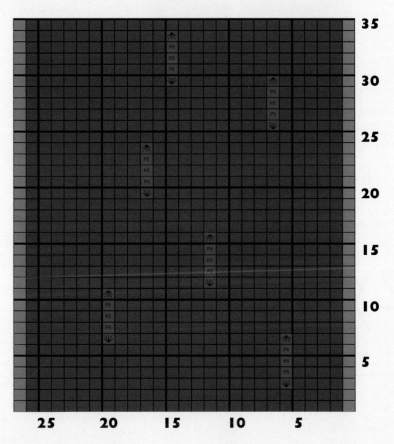

Dec from 5 sts to 1 st

Inc from 1 st to 5 sts

P5 Purl these 5 sts

K5 Knit these 5 sts

St st (in black)

St st (in black) for larger size only

Reminiscent of fireworks, these vivid and vibrant gloves will add a sparkle to any outfit. Children can flip the tops back to play and forward to keep warm!

Snazzy flip-tops

Size

To fit child aged 10–14years
Circumference 7in (17.5cm)
Length (adjustable) 8½in (21.5cm)

Tension

23 sts and 34 rows to 4in (10cm) over patt using 4mm needles (be careful not to pull in the Fairisle rows)
Use larger or smaller needles to achieve correct tension

Materials

Stylecraft Special DK 100% acrylic (304m/332yds per 100g ball)
1 x 100g ball in 1011 Midnight (MC)
Wendy Peter Pan 55% nylon 45% courtelle (170m/186yds per 100g ball)
1 x 50g ball in 1320 Tartan (CC)
A set each 3.25mm (UK10:US3) and 4mm (UK8:US6) double-pointed needles

Pattern notes

Fairisle pattern repeat
Row 1: K1 in MC, k1 in CC, k2 in MC.
Row 2: K3 in CC, k1 in MC.
Row 3: K1 in MC, k1 in CC, k2 in MC.

Stripe sequence
3 rounds Fairisle rep foll chart, 6 rounds st st in MC, * 4 rounds st st in CC, 6 rounds st st in in MC *, 3 rounds Fairisle rep foll chart, 6 rounds st st in MC.

Method

These mittens have an optional flip-top, and a glove version is also given within the instructions. They are made starting at the wrist with a 2 x 2 rib, then with Fairisle and stripes in a variegated yarn against a navy-blue background.

First mitten

Hand section
With 3.25mm needles cast on 42 sts and work in 2 x 2 rib as folls:
6 rounds in MC.
3 rounds in CC.
2 rounds in MC.
3 rounds in CC.
6 rounds in MC.
Change to 4mm needles and work 1 round st st in MC.

Begin stripe sequence
at the same time, work as folls:
Rounds 1–3: K1 in MC, work Fairisle patt reps to last st, k1 in MC.
Change to st st and work 6 rounds in MC.

Thumb gusset
Round 1: K20, (M1), k20.
Round 2 (and every alt row): Knit.
Round 3: K20, (M1R, k1, M1L), k20.
Round 5: K20, (M1R, k3, M1L), k20.
Cont in this way, inc 2 sts on every round until the round (M1R, K13, M1L) has been worked.
Next round: Work without shaping.
Place central 15 thumb sts on a holder. 40 sts.
Cont in stripe sequence until work measures 1in (2.5cm) from beg of thumb gusset and 5½in (14cm) from the start. This should take you to the base of the fingers; adjust length here if necessary.

Change to 3.25mm needles and work 4 rows rib in MC.
Cast off loosely, making sure the rib fits comfortably round the hand.

Thumb

Place the 15 sts left for the thumb on 4mm dpns.
Keeping stripe sequence the same as for the hand, work as folls:
Round 1: With MC, inc 1 st at base and work 1 round. 16 sts.
Work 3 Fairisle patt rounds.
Continue in MC until thumb measures 1¾in (4.5cm) or required length.
Next round: (k2tog) to end.
Work 1 more round and pull yarn through sts to complete.
Note: For gloves, work as 'Child's play' glove in the 4-needle version (see page 14), adjusting finger lengths if necessary.

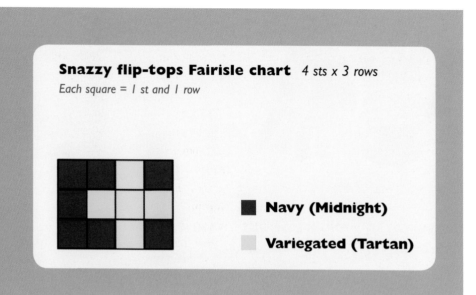

Snazzy flip-tops Fairisle chart *4 sts x 3 rows*

Each square = 1 st and 1 row

■ **Navy (Midnight)**

□ **Variegated (Tartan)**

Decrease for top

Keeping patt correct, work as folls:

Next round: * (K2tog tbl) to 2 sts before halfway marker, k2tog, rep from * once more after marker. 40 sts (20 each side of marker).

Next round: Work without shaping. Work last 2 rows once more. 36 sts (18 sts each side of marker). Now dec every row until 10 sts rem on each side of the marker. Cast off using the 3-needle method.

Second mitten

Work as for first mitten, making sure the thumb is on the opposite side when picking up the back sts. The beg of the circle, when formed, will be on the thumb end of the right mitten. On the left mitten it will be on the opposite end.

Making up

Darn in ends and secure edge of flip-top below rib rows. Leave under a damp cloth overnight.

Fliptop

With MC pick up (without knitting) 21 sts across back **below** rib and leave on a dpn.

On another 4mm dpn, cast on 21 sts, then cont (with RS of the back of mitten facing) across picked-up sts, inc 1 st in the first and last of the picked-up sts. 44 sts. *Do not form circle yet.*

Next 2 rows: Knit on 2 needles over these 44 sts.

Now join into a circle round the rib top of the mitten using 4mm dpns.

Work 3 rounds in st st.

Cont in st st marking the centre of the round (22 sts each side) and resume stripe sequence from * to *. Work 3 rounds in Fairisle.

Note: The 2 extra sts mean that you will need to add an extra 'k1' in MC at the beg of round and at the halfway point in order to keep the patt in line with the main part of the hand. At the same time on row 2 of patt or the desired length (about ¾in [2cm] less than finished length) start to dec for top.

There is nothing sartorially square about these elegant and cozy gloves. Effortlessly stylish, they add a touch of sophistication to any winter wardrobe.

Lace squares

Size

To fit small to medium woman
Circumference 7in (18cm) approx
Finger lengths adjustable

Tension

23 sts and 26 rows to 4in (10cm) over patt using
4mm needles
Use larger or smaller needles to achieve correct tension

Materials

Rowan Tapestry 70% wool 30% soybean protein fibre
(120m/131yds per 50g ball)
2 x 50g balls in 177 Lead Mine (grey mix)
A pair of 4mm (UK8:US6) needles
A set each 3mm (UK11:US2–3) and 4mm (UK8:US6)
double-pointed needles

Pattern notes

This glove is stretchy and should fit a small to average-size woman. The pattern dictates the number of stitches and rows in the hand up to the fingers, but finger lengths are adjustable.

Method

These gloves begin with an optional frill at the wrist, then a 2 x 2 rib. The hand is worked in a lace square pattern as a 20-row repeat. The fingers are worked in 2 x 2 rib.

Gloves

Frill (optional)

Using 4mm needles, cast on 173 sts. I found it easier to knit the frill on 2 long needles rather than dpns.

Row 1: (RS) K1, (skpo) to end. 87 sts.
Row 2: (WS) P1 (p2tog) to end. 44 sts.

Rib

Note: If not working frill, begin here.
Cast on 44 sts divided evenly between 3 x 3mm dpns.
Work in 2 x 2 rib for 1in (2.5cm) if you have worked a frill or for 2in (5cm) if there is no frill, dec 2 sts on last row. 42 sts.

Right hand

Change to 4mm dpns and work over 42 sts as folls:

Pattern

Round 1: (k3, yf, skpo, k2, p7) to end.
Round 2: (k7, p7) to end.
Round 3: (k1, k2tog, yf, k1, yf, skpo, k1, p7) to end.
Round 5: (k2tog, yf, k3, yf, skpo, p7) to end.
Round 7: (k2, yf, s1, k2tog, psso, yf, k2, p7) to end.
Round 8: (k7, p7) to end
Round 9: As row 1.
Round 10: As row 2.
Now move the squares so round 11 starts (p7, k3, yf, skpo, k2).
Round 11: (p7, k3, yf, skpo, k2), to end.
Cont to row 20 as set.
These 20 rows form the patt. Rep them once more. *At the same time start to shape the thumb gusset on row 3 as folls:*

Thumb shaping

Note: Although the work is still in the round on dpns, the thumb shaping is set out in rows to differentiate it from the rounds required to work the pattern:
Round 1: K21, M1 (by picking up loop between sts), work 21 sts to end.
Round 2: Work even (without inc), knitting the newly-made st.
Round 3: (k21, M1L, k3, M1R), work to end.
Round 4 (and all alternate rows): As row 2.
Round 5: (k21, M1R, k5 M1L) work to end.
Cont as set, adding 2 sts every other row until the row (k21, M1R, k15, M1L, k21) has been worked.
Work in patt until the fourth row of squares has been completed. 40 rows.
Note: On the last row, M1 at each end of each purl square. 48 sts for fingers.
Place all sts on a thread except for last 5 sts at beginning and 5 sts at end of round. Place these 10 sts on 2 dpns.
Note: RH fingers are picked up palm facing, left hand back facing. The fingers are worked in rib using 4mm needles.

Little finger

Cast on and purl 2 sts, k2, p2, k1. 12 sts. Work for 2in (5cm), then work top of finger.

* **Next rnd:** (k2tog) to end.
Next rnd: Knit.
Break off yarn and pull end through all sts to close *.

Third (ring) finger

Place 6 sts from front of waste yarn on one dpn, and 6 sts from back of waste yarn on a second dpn.
Pick up and purl 2 sts at beg of rnd, (k2, p2, k2) on first needle, pick up and purl 2 sts from base of last finger, (k2, p2, k2) to end.
Work in rib as set for 2⅓in (6cm). then work top * to *.

Second finger

As for third finger but work 2½in (6.5cm), then work top * to *.

Forefinger (first finger)

Put rem 14 sts on dpns, pick up and purl 2 sts from base of second finger. Work in rib for 2¼in (5.5cm) then work top * to *.

Thumb

Place sts from waste yarn on dpns, inc at the glove end. 16 sts.
Work in rib for 2⅓in (6cm).
Next round: (k2tog) to end. 8 sts.
Next round: With 3mm needles, knit to end.
Break off yarn and pull end through all sts to close.

Left hand

The thumb of these gloves is central, so it will probably not matter much if you make both gloves the same. To be strictly symmetrical, however, begin the pattern for the left glove on round 11. The finger sts are picked up back facing.

Making up

Darn in any loose ends and leave under a damp cloth overnight.

Made with ecological yarn these mittens with their delightful llama design
are certain to become a favourite among animal lovers. Practical
and pretty, they'll keep your hands really warm.

Llama mittens

Size

To fit adult (man or woman)
Circumference 8¾(8)in [22(20.5)cm]
Length (adjustable) 9¾(9)in [25(23)cm]

Tension

22 sts and 26 rows to 4in (10cm) over st st using
4.5mm needles
23.5 sts and 28 rows to 4in (10cm) over st st using
4mm needles
Use larger or smaller needles to achieve correct tension

Materials

Uppingham Yarns Ecologica Pura Lana 100% ecological wool
(85m/93yds per 50g ball)
2 x 50g balls in 605 Light Grey Marl (MC)
1 x 50g ball in 152 Earth (CC)
A pair each 3.75mm and 4.5mm needles for man's size
A pair each 3.5mm and 4mm needles for woman's size

Special techniques

Intarsia

2-needle cast-off

Pattern notes

Twist 2 Knit next 2 sts tog without removing them from the needle, then knit the first st again, and slip both sts on to the right needle.

Method

These mittens are worked on two needles beginning with a twisted-rib cuff. The main mitten is then worked with a Fairisle border above and below the intarsia llama pattern. The thumb and mitten top is then completed.

First mitten

With 3.75 (3.5)mm needles and MC, cast on 48 sts.

Work twisted rib as folls:

Row 1: K1, (p2, k2) to end, k1.

Row 2: P1, (k2, p2) to last st, p1.

Row 3: K1, (p2, twist 2) to last st, k1.

Row 4: As row 2.

These 4 rows form the twisted rib pattern. Rep rows 1–4 until work measures 2in (5cm).

Main part

Change to 4.5(4)mm needles and st st. Knit 2(1) rows.

Work 3-row border patt (see chart).

Work 3 rows in st st then begin to work llama chart.

Note: Work llama in intarsia, not Fairisle (see Techniques, page 149), beg chart 2 sts in – i.e. for first row work 4MC, 2CC, 1MC, 2CC, 5MC, 2CC, 1MC, 2CC, 3MC. At the same time, beg to work thumb gusset on row 7 (5) of pattern.

Thumb gusset

Row 1: K2, work chart, k2 (place halfway marker), k3, M1, k21. 49 sts.

Row 2: Cont to foll chart as set (p row).

Row 3: K2, cont to foll chart as set, k2, k3 (M1R, k1, m1L), k21.

Row 4: As row 2.

Row 5: K1, cont to foll chart, k2, k3 (M1R, k3, M1L), k21.

Cont with rows 4–5, inc 2 sts on each row until the row M1R, k15, M1L(M1R, k13, M1L) has been worked.

Thumb

P36, turn, M1R, inc by knitting into the front and back of the next st (kf and b), k15(13), kf and b, M1L. 21(19) sts.

Turn, p21(19), cont in st st on these 21(19) sts for 2¼ (2)in [5.5(5)cm] or ½in (1cm) less than desired length.

Next row: (K2tog, k1) to last st, k1. 14(13) sts.

P 1 row.

Man's size: (k2tog) 7 times.

Woman's size: (k2tog) 3 times, k1, (k2tog) 3 times.

Both sizes: Break off yarn and pull end through all 7 sts to close.

Rejoin yarn to base of thumb (purl side facing) and complete purl row.

Work to end of Llama chart, approx 8¾in(8)in [22.5(20)cm].

Decrease for top

Note: Adjust length here if necessary.

Row 1: K1, * (sl, k1, psso), k19, k2tog (to reach centre marker), rep from * once, k1.

Row 2: Purl.

Rep last 2 rows once, then the first row again.

Next row: P1, (p2tog, p13, p2tog tbl) twice, p1.

Work row 1 again.

Rep until 24 sts rem.

Divide into 2 sets of 12 sts and cast off using the 3-needle method.

Second mitten

As for first mitten with the following adjustment: On row 7(5) set thumb gusset as folls: (k21, M1, k3, k24). Work as first thumb gusset. For thumb, p44(42), turn and work as first thumb.

Set llama pattern as folls: k21, (M1, k3, M1), k3 (the halfway mark), k2, work chart, k2.

Note: Both llamas face the same way. If you want the second to face the other way, start from the other side of chart.

Making up

As this is a wool yarn, press seams on WS with medium iron and damp cloth. Leave under a damp cloth overnight.

Llama *20 sts x 34 rows*

Each square = I st and I row

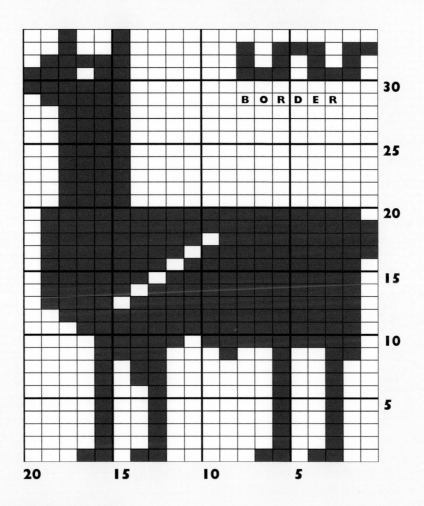

■ **Dark brown (Earth)**

□ **Light brown (Grey Marl)**

For something different, why not try making these long, woolly mittens for maximum warmth in the long winter months. This pattern is easier than it looks, so why not give it a go?

Mock-rib mittens

Size

Size small or average
Will stretch from approx 6¼–7(7–8)in [16–18(18–20)cm]

Tension

This is difficult to gauge because the pattern is stretchy, but 3 patt reps on 5mm needles measure approx 2¾in (7cm) (unstretched)
Instead of a tension square, cast on 35 sts and work in the round for about 3 patt reps on 5mm needles
Use larger or smaller needles to achieve correct tension

Materials

Wendy Zena Aran 18% alpaca 24% wool 50% polyacrylic 8% polyamide (100m/109yds per 50g ball)
2 x 50g balls in 1553 Iris Star
A set each 4mm (UK8:US6) and 5mm (UK6:US8) double-pointed needles

Pattern notes

The thumbs on the smaller size are not precisely centred: they have to be set over the pattern (C3, p2, C3) so they do not pull on the palm.

Special abbreviation

Cross 3 sts (C3)

Insert point of right needle into the third of the 3 knit sts. Knit the st, but do not remove it from needle. Now knit the front st and remove from left needle. Knit the next st (the centre of the 3 knit sts) and slip it and the 3rd st off the needle tog.

Note: This is effectively the same as placing 2 sts on a cable needle, then working (k1, k2) from the cable needle, but is quicker and easier. It may be easier to insert the right needle p-wise into the third st, pull it towards you, then remove the right needle and knit the st.

Method

This long mitten begins with a (p2, k3) rib at the forearm which leads into the mock-rib pattern stitch. The thumb and hand openings are worked in rib before casting off.

Mittens

On 4mm needles cast on 35(40) sts.

Note: This should be long enough to go around your wrist: if it is tight, cast on using 5mm needles instead.

Set rib as folls: (p2, k3) to end.

Work a total of 8 rows in rib.

Change to 5mm needles and work in patt as folls:

Rounds 1, 2 & 4: (RS) (p2, k3) to end.

Round 3: (p2, C3) to end.

These 4 rows set the pattern. Rep for approx 8in (20cm), ending with row 1, then divide sts for thumb as folls:

Small size

Left hand: Work 12 sts, work the next sts (k3, p2, k3) and place on a safety pin, work to end of round.

Right hand: Work 17 sts, work the next sts (k3, p2, k3) and put onto a safety pin, work to end of round.

Average size

Right hand: Work 22 sts, work the next sts (k3, p2, k3) and place on a safety pin, work to end of round.

Left hand: Work 12 sts, work the next (k3, p2, k3) and put onto safety pin, work to end of round.

Both sizes

Cont to work in patt, casting on 8 sts over the sts held on the safety pin. Work a further 1½(2)in [4(5)cm] or required length, ending with a row 1.

Change to 4mm needles and work 5 rows in (p2, k3) rib.

Cast off loosely (use larger needles if necessary).

Work thumb

With 4mm needles, pick up 2 sts at right side of thumb sts on pin for fourchette (see Techniques, page 144). Work (k3, p2, k3) across pin sts, pick up 2 sts and pick up 8 sts across top of thumb gusset or fourchette.

Next round: P2 (fourchette), k3, p2, k3, p2 (fourchette), k3, p2, k3. Work 8 rounds in total as set, then cast off making sure the thumb fits easily. For larger size, cast off using 5mm needles.

Making up

Darn in ends and tidy up the thumb gussets. Leave under a damp cloth overnight.

With their wonderful array of colours and soft textures, these gloves will quickly draw a crowd of interested admirers. This was my most expensive yarn. What can I say? I fell in love!

Lovely luxury

Size

To fit adult
This is a very stretchy pattern and the circumference will fit most hands

Tension

26 sts and 33 rows to 4in (10cm) over lace patt using 4mm needles
Use larger or smaller needles to achieve correct tension

Materials

Noro Cashmere Island 30% cashmere 60% wool 10% nylon (100m/110yds per 50g hank)
1 x 50g hank in Colour 12 for fingerless mittens
2 x 50g hanks in Colour 12 for gloves
A set each 3.25mm (UK10:US3) and 4mm (UK8:US6) double-pointed needles

Pattern notes
Rib eyelet pattern
Rounds 1–3: (k3, p2) to end.
Round 4: (k2tog, yo, k1, p2) to end.
Round 5–7: (k3, p2) to end.
Round 8: (k1, yo, skpo, p2) to end.

Lace pattern (6-st rep)
Rounds 1–2: (k5, p1) to end.
Round 3: (yo, skpo, p1, k2tog, yo, k1) to end.
Rounds 4–6: (k2, p1, k3) to end.
Round 7: (k2tog, yo, k1, yo, skpo, p1) to end.
Round 8: As row 1.
These 8 rows form the pattern.

Method
This looks like Aran but is actually a lace pattern. The mittens, which are worked in the round throughout, begin at the wrist with a lacy rib pattern, followed by the hand in the main pattern. Short finger shapings complete the mittens.

Mittens
With 3.25mm needles cast on 45 sts and work in rib patt, beg with row 2. Work 20 rows, ending on row 5 of patt.
Next round (inc): Keeping rib correct, (rib 15, M1) twice, rib 14, M1, k1. 48 sts.
Change to 4mm needles and work in lace patt for hand. *At the same time,* begin to work thumb gusset on row 3. *(Note: The lace pattern is adapted to give the 'best fit' within the gusset stitches.)* Work 24 sts, M2 (as M1 but knit into the front and back of picked-up yarn), work 24 sts. Place a marker each side of the 2 made sts and knit them on the next 3 rows.
Inc 2 gusset sts every 4 rows as folls:
Round 7 (inc): Work 24 sts, M1R, k2, M1L, work 24 sts
Work next 3 rows, knitting gusset sts.
Round 11 (inc): Work to marker, pick up loop as if to M1R but do not knit, leave loop on right needle, sl next 4 sts, pick up loop as if to M1L but do not knit. Slip this loop, the previous 4 sts and M1R loop on to left needle. Work in lace pattern over these sts: yo, skpo, p1, k2tog, yo, k1. 6 sts inside gusset marker. Work to end.
Work in patt for 3 rounds.
Round 15 (inc): Work to marker, M1R, k2tog, yo, k1, yo, skpo, p1, M1L, work to end keeping patt correct. 8 gusset sts.
Next 3 rounds: Work sts within gusset as (k1, k5, p1, k1).
Round 19 (inc): Work to marker, M1R, k1, yo, skpo, p1, k2tog, k1, k1, M1L. 10 sts.
Next 3 rounds: Work sts within gusset as (k2, k2, p1, k3, k2).
Round 23 (inc): Work to marker, M1R but do not knit, s10, M1L but do not knit, then slip gusset sts and the newly-made

sts back on to left needle and work as folls: (k2tog, yo, k1, yo, skpo, p1) twice. 12 sts in gusset.

Next 3 rounds: Work in patt.

Round 27: (Inc) Work to marker, M1R, (yo, skpo, p1, k2tog, yo, k1) twice, M1L. 14 sts.

Next round: Place these 14 gusset sts on a safety pin or coloured thread for thumb. 48 sts on needle.

Cont in patt until work measures 4in (10cm) or desired length.

Break off yarn and place all sts on a coloured thread ready for fingers.

Little finger

Take first 6 sts onto a dpn and last 6 sts onto another dpn. Inc 2 sts at thumb end. *

Working the extra sts as knit throughout, cont in patt as set for the hand for ½in (1cm).

Work in 1x1 rib for 1 row.

Cast off loosely in rib. *

Third and second fingers

Take 6 sts from front and back of thread, inc 2 sts at front and knit, patt 6 sts, pick up 2 sts from base of last finger, patt 6 sts. Work * to *.

Forefinger (first finger)

Using rem sts, pick up 2 sts from base of last finger and knit. Work rem 12 sts in patt * to *.

Thumb

Take 14 sts from thread. Pick up and knit 2 sts from base of thumb. Work in patt as folls: K2, patt 12, k2.

Work * to *.

Variation (gloves)

Cont until fingers and thumb are desired length, then complete as folls:

Next row: Knit.

Next row: (k2tog) to end.

Next row: Knit.

Break off yarn and pull end through sts.

Making up

Darn in ends and leave under a damp cloth overnight.

These absolutely stunning birds are connected with both the Roman Goddess Juno and the Hindu Goddess Parvati. The mix of blue and green echoes the dominant colours in the birds' feathers and highlights out their finer points.

A pride of peacocks

Size

To fit average woman (finger lengths can be adjusted)
Circumference above thumb 8in (20cm) approx
Little finger 2in (5cm)
Third finger 2½in (6.5cm)
Second finger 2¾in (7cm)
First finger 2¼in (6cm)

Tension

24 sts and 32 rows to 4in (10cm) over st st using 4mm
needles and Sirdar Click
Use larger or smaller needles to achieve correct tension

Materials

Cygnet Superwash Wool DK 100% pure new wool
(104m/114yds) per 50g ball)
1 x 50g ball 2150 Tartan Green
Patons Diploma Gold DK 55% wool 25% acrylic 20% nylon
(104m/114yds) per 50g ball)
1 x 50g ball 6170 Royal
Sirdar Click DK 70% Acrylic 30% Wool (150m/164yd per 50g ball)
1 x 50g ball in 0144 Downy
A set each 3.25mm (UK10:US3) and 4mm (UK8:US6) needles
Stitch markers

Special techniques

Fairisle

MIR, MIL

Method

These gloves begin with 2 x 2 rib at the wrist. The main part begins and ends with a combination of stocking stitch in a neutral shade and a Fairisle zig-zag. Seam stitches are added to the central area and the peacock section is worked in intarsia. Fingers and thumb are then made and tipped with contrast colour.

Gloves

With 3.25mm needles and Royal, cast on 48 sts. Distribute sts over 3 dpns and work 1 round of 2 x 2 rib. Change to Tartan Green and work rib for 2¼in (6cm). On the final row inc 1 st as folls:

Right glove: Work 27, M1, keeping rib correct, work to end. 49 sts.

Left glove: Work 21, M1, keeping rib correct, work to end. 49 sts.

Both gloves

Change to 4mm needles and Downy. Work 5 rows of chart. On row 6 of chart beg thumb gusset as folls:

Right glove: Work 27 sts, (MIR, k1, MIL), work to end.

Left glove: Work 21 sts, (MIR, k1, MIL), work to end.

Both gloves

Work one row even (still foll chart).

Next and every alt round: Inc the gusset (as set) by 2 sts. The shaping of the next inc row will be (M1, k3, M1). Cont until the inc round (MIR, k7, MIL) has been worked.

Next round: Place 17 sts on a safety pin for thumb, k to end of round. 48 sts.

At the same time, set peacock and divide for intarsia.

Right glove: Add 2 seam sts at beg of next row (see techniques), PM, beg from RS work 24 sts of row 1 of peacock chart, work to last st, PM, add 2 seam sts. Foll chart, work the intarsia peacock back and forth on 3 needles.

When you have finished working the peacock, dec the 2 seam sts at each edge (outside markers) and join up the round. 48 sts.

Complete chart in Fairisle, then work 3 more rounds st st in Downy to complete hand.

Left glove: Place markers as for right glove, count 27 sts and work as for right glove but begin from left side.

Both gloves

Note: Use separate lengths of yarn for body and tail. Peacocks should be placed on the back of the gloves facing away from the thumb. RH fingers are worked with palm facing, LH fingers with back facing.

Fingers

Work 1 row in Green, break off yarns. Place the first 18 sts on a thread or holder, the next 6 sts on a dpn, the foll 6 sts on another dpn, and the rem 18 sts on another thread or holder.

Little finger

Inc 2 sts, work 12 sts. 14 sts.

Work in rounds until finger measures 1¾in (4.5cm).

* Change to Royal and work 3 rounds.

Next round: Change to 3.25mm needles and work (k2tog) to end. Work 1 round.

Break off yarn and thread yarn through all sts to fasten off *.

Third (ring) finger

Place next 5 sts from back and front threads on a dpn, inc 2 sts, k5, pick up 2 sts from base of little finger. 14 sts.

Work for 2¼in (6cm) then * to *.

Second finger

Take next 6 sts from back and front, inc 2 sts, k6, pick up 2 sts, k6 sts. 16 sts.

Work for 2½in (6.5cm) then * to *.

Forefinger (first finger)

Pick up 2 sts from base of second finger and join rem sts. 16 sts.

Work for 2¼in (5.5cm) then * to *.

Thumb

Pick up 2 sts at base of thumb, knit sts
from thread to form a round of 19 sts.
Work for 1¾in (4.5cm), then change
to Royal for 2 rounds.

Next round: (k1, k2tog) to last st, k1.
13 sts.

Knit 1 round.

Change to 3.25mm needles. (k2tog)
3 times, k1, (k2tog) 3 times.

Knit 1 round.

Break off yarn and pull through sts
to fasten off.

Making up

Join side seam using mattress stitch
or back stitch (see Techniques, page 152).
Tidy fingers and thumb gussets.

Cover with a damp cloth, place a
polythene sheet on top and then
a book, and leave overnight.

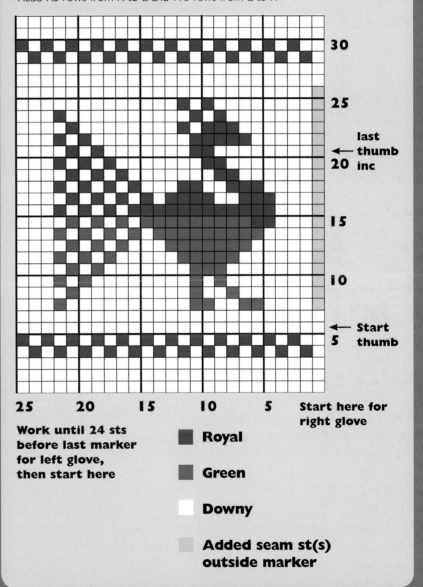

A pride of peacocks chart *25 sts x 32 rows*

Each square = 1 st and 1 row

Read RS rows from R to L and WS rows from L to R

30

25

← last
thumb
20 inc

15

10

← Start
5 thumb

25   20   15   10   5   Start here for
right glove

Work until 24 sts
before last marker
for left glove,
then start here

Royal

Green

Downy

Added seam st(s)
outside marker

A unisex glove, perfect for sharing with your loved one, but make sure you get there first on those hand-numbing days! This fun glove explores the use of different textures and contrasts of colours while remaining practical.

Sampler gloves

Size

To fit M/L man (S/M woman)

Circumference approx 8(6⅔)in [20(17)cm]

Top of Pattern 1 to fingers: approx 4(3¼)in [10(8)cm]

Measurements are approximate because the tension varies a little between patterns

Tension

As each pattern varies slightly, use an average overall tension of 24 sts and 30 rows over 4in (10cm) in st st as a guide

Materials

Cygnet Superwash DK pure new wool

(104m/110yds per 50g ball)

1 x 50g ball in 2284 Denim

1 x 50g ball in 4315 Taupe

1 x 50g ball in 0217 Black

1 x 50g ball in 0298 Cranberry

A set each 3.5mm (UK9–10:US4) and 4mm (UK8:US6) double-pointed needles

Method

This fun glove explores different textures and colours. It begins at the wrist with a 2 x 2 rib, followed by the hand in a variety of patterns and colour combinations. Fingers and thumb are then made. Both gloves are the same.

Gloves

With 3.5mm needles and Black, cast on 48(40) sts.
Work in 2 x 2 rib for 2⅓ in (6cm).
Change to 4mm needles and join in Cranberry.
Rep patterns 1–5 in order given, but omitting patt 2 for smaller size only.

Pattern 1 (both sizes)

Round 1: Knit.
Round 2: Purl.
Join in Taupe.
Next 2 rounds: (k2 Taupe, k2 Cranberry) to end.
Next round: Knit, using Cranberry.
Next round: Purl, using Cranberry.

Pattern 2 (larger size only)

Round 1: Knit, using Denim.
Work 5 rows from pattern chart using Denim as MC and Taupe as CC.
Next round: Knit, using Denim.
Next round: Knit, still uing Denim. At the same time, begin gusset (see right).

Pattern 3 (both sizes)

Round 1: (Knit into first st but do not remove from left needle, yo, knit into st again, remove these sts to right needle, p3) to end.
Round 2: (k3, p3) to end.
Round 3: As round 2.
Round 4: (k3tog, p3) to end.
Work 2 rounds in Denim.

Gusset

Using Denim, work 24(20) sts, place marker, M1, place marker, work to end always starting the patt again as at the beg of the round.
Next and foll alt round: Purl the st(s) between markers.
On round 2 of Pattern 3 (cobnuts) work to marker, (M1R, p1, M1L).
On round 4 of Pattern 3 work to marker, (M1R, p3, M1L). 5 gusset sts.
On first knit round of Denim, knit the sts between markers.
On second knit row of Denim work bet markers as (M1R, k5, M1). 7 sts.

Pattern 4

Rep the Fairisle pattern chart but using Black as MC and Cranberry as CC.
At the same time, cont gusset as folls:
Round 1: (Fairisle within markers, no inc) work as (k1 st in Black, k5 sts in Cranberry, k1 st in Black). 7 gusset sts.

Round 2: work as (M1R in Black, k2 sts in Black, k3 sts in Cranberry, k2 sts in Black, M1L in Black). 9 gusset sts.
Round 3: (no inc) work as (k4 sts in Black, k1 st in Cranberry, k4 sts in Black).
Round 4: work as (M1R Black, k3 sts in Black, k3 sts in Red, k3 sts in Black, M1L in Black. 11 sts.
Round 5: (no inc) work as (k3 sts in Black, k5 sts in Red, k3 sts in Black.
Next round: Knit using Denim, working gusset as (M1, k11, M1). 13 sts.
Next round: Still using Denim, work even across gusset.
Change to Taupe.
Next round: Knit, then work last gusset inc as (M1, k13, M1).
Next round: Purl, then place the 15 gusset sts on a safety pin or thread 48(40) sts.
Next 2 rounds: (k2 sts in Cranberry, k2 sts in Taupe) to end.
Next round: Knit, using Taupe.
Next round: Purl, using Taupe.

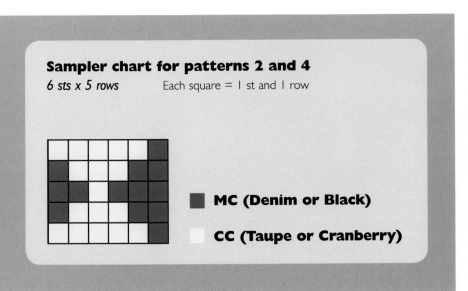

Sampler chart for patterns 2 and 4

6 sts x 5 rows   Each square = 1 st and 1 row

■ **MC (Denim or Black)**

□ **CC (Taupe or Cranberry)**

Third and second fingers

Put next 6(5) sts from back onto one DPN, next 6(5) sts from front onto another.

Inc 2, k6(5), pick up 2 from base of previous finger, k6(5). 16(14)sts. Work for 2¾(2⅓)in [7(6)cm] for third finger and 3¼(2½)in [8(6.5)cm] for second finger, then * to *.

Forefinger (first finger)

Pick up 2 sts from base of previous finger, then k rem 4(12)sts. 16(14) sts. Work for 2¾(2⅓)in [7(6)cm], then * to *.

Thumb

Place 15 thumb sts on dpns. Pick up 3(2) sts at base of thumb. Work for 2(1¾)in [5(4.5)cm].

Next round: (k2tog) to last st, end k1(0).

Next round: Knit.

Next round: (k2tog) to last st, end k1(0).

Making up

Darn in ends and leave under a damp cloth overnight.

Pattern 5

Row 1: (p3tog without slipping sts from left needle, k3tog into same sts, p3tog again into same sts, then slip sts off left needle), p1. Rep to end. 48(40) sts.

Round 2: Knit.

Round 3: (k3, p1) to end.

Rep rounds 1–3 until glove is almost the desired length.

Note: Adjust length here as required.

Next round: Knit, using Taupe.

Next round: Purl, using Taupe.

Place all sts on a thread for fingers, with ends at little finger end.

Little finger

Place 5(4) sts from back and 5(4) sts from front on dpns. Inc 2, k5(4) sts from first dpn, M1, k5(4) sts from second dpn. 13(11) sts.

Work for 2⅓(2)in [6(5)cm].

* (K2tog) to last st, k one round with 3.5mm needles, break off yarn and pull end through sts to close *.

This simple yet effective pattern is far easier than it looks, and its woven effect is neither masculine nor feminine in its two-tone boldness. Beware: these gloves may cause arguments!

Caught in the slips

Size

To fit adult man (woman)
Circumference above thumb 8¼ (7)in [21(18)cm]
Wrist to fingers 4(3½)in [10(9)cm]

Tension

27 sts and 36 rounds to 4in (10cm) over patt using 4.5mm needles
24 sts and 32 rounds to 4in (10cm) over st st on 4mm needles
Use larger or smaller needles to achieve correct tension

Materials

Cygnet Superwash Wool DK 100% pure new wool (104m/114yds per 50g ball)
2 x 50g balls in 2153 Navy (MC)
1 x 50g ball in 4315 Taupe (CC)
A set each 3.25mm (UK10:US3), 4mm (UK8:US6) and 4.5mm (UK7:US7) double-pointed needles

Special abbreviations

Ss1 Slip stitch 1 (yf, slip 1 st p-wise, yb)
This gives a bar across the stitch below
on the RS of the work.

Pattern notes

This slip-stitch pattern uses only one
colour in any round: stitches are slipped
on one round and knitted on the next.
The first round of each colour always
begins with a knit stitch and the second
with a slip stitch. After the first round
of a colour the loops on the needle
will be in alternate colours; after a
second round they will all be the same.
On rounds 1 and 3 always bring the
new colour up under the old one; on
rounds 2 and 4 take it round the other
colour. Work 2 sts, then pull firmly on
both yarns to close the circle. Pull on the
second stitch when you change needles.

Method

The gloves start at the wrist with a
1 x 1 rib. The main part is worked in
the round in a two-colour slip stitch
sequence, then the fingers and thumb
are worked in stocking stitch. Pattern
is shown in rows for clarity.

Gloves

With 3.25mm needles and MC, cast
on 48 sts and work in 1 x 1 rib for
2¾(2¼)in [7(6)cm], inc on final round
for man's size only as folls: (k4, M1) to
last 4 sts, k4. 58(48) sts.
Join in CC, change to 4.5mm needles.
and beg patt.
Row 1: Using CC, (ss1, k1) to end.
Row 2: Using CC, (k1, ss1) to end.
Row 3: Using MC, (ss1, k1) to end.
Row 4: Using MC, (k1, ss1) to end.
These 4 rows form patt and are
repeated. *At the same time,* inc for
thumb gusset on round 2 as folls:
Work 28(24) sts, M2 in Taupe by
picking up thread between sts and
knitting into the front and back of it,
place marker each side of these 2 new
sts; cont in patt to end (these sts will
be worked in patt on foll rounds).
Round 8: Work to first marker, M2R
(as M1R but knit into front and back of
picked-up thread), ss1, k1 across 2 sts
bet markers, M2L (as before).
Every foll 8th round: Work up to
marker, (M2R [ss1, k1] across gusset sts,
M2L) until there are 18 sts in the
gusset for man's size (M2, k14, M2) or
14 sts for woman's size (M2, k10, M2).
Work 1 round, then place these sts
on a safety pin or coloured thread.
Cont on rem sts until work measures

4(3½)in [10(9)cm] or length required
from wrist to fingers, ending with
a round 4 (MC).
Change to 4mm needles and knit
1 round in MC over all sts.
Place all the sts on a thread with ends
at beg and end of round (little finger
end) and lay glove flat.

Little finger

Pick up the last 6(5) sts from beg
of thread and the last 6(5) sts from
end of the thread, inc 2. Work in
the round on these 14(12) sts for
2⅓(2)in [6(5)cm].
Work top on next 2 rounds as folls:
Next round: *(k2tog) to end.
Next round: Knit, using 3.25mm
needles for a neater finish.
Break off yarn and pull end through sts
to close *.

Third (ring) finger

Take next 7(6) sts from front and back
of thread as before. Beg from the end
away from the little finger inc 1(2) sts,
k7(6), pick up 1(2) sts from base of
little finger, knit the other 7(6) sts. Join
the 16 sts into a round and work until
finger measures 2¾in(2⅓in)in [7(6)cm].
Work top as for * to * of little finger.

Second finger

As third finger but work to 3¼(2½)in [8(6.5)cm] length.

Forefinger (first finger)

Place rem 16(14) sts on needles, then pick up 1(2) st(s) from base of second finger. Work on these 17(16) sts for 2¾(2¼)in [7(5.5)cm].

Work top

Man's glove: (k2tog) to last st, k1. 9 sts.

Woman's glove: Work * to * as for little finger.

Break off yarn and pull end through sts to close.

Thumb

Place the 18(14) thumb sts on needles; pick up 2 sts from base. 20 (16) sts.

Both sizes: Work even for 2 rounds.

Next round (man's size only): K2tog at beg and end of round (where thumb joins hand). 18 sts.

Both sizes: Work on these 18(16) sts for 2¼(2)in [5.5(5)cm].

Work top * to *. of little finger

Making up

Darn in yarn inside top of fingers and neaten areas between fingers. Rep for thumb. Darn in ends and leave under a damp cloth overnight.

Nature lovers won't be able to resist these beautiful and uniquely textured gloves reflecting the scenery of frosty rural walks. Get knitting, so next time you go out walking you can blend into the environment!

Textured heather

Size

To fit average woman(man)
Circumference 7½(8)in [19(20.5)cm]
Wrist to fingers 3½(4⅓)in [9(11)cm]

Tension

29 sts and 32 rows to 4in (10cm) over patt using
3.5mm needles
Use larger or smaller needles to achieve correct tension

Materials

Sirdar Click DK 70% Acrylic 30% Wool (150m/164yds
per 50g ball)
1 × 50g ball in 0131 Heather
1 × 50g ball in 0128 Tarn
A set each 3.25mm (UK10:US3) and 3.5mm (UK9–10:US4)
double-pointed needles

Special abbreviations

(Yf, k2 psso) = Yarn forward, knit 2, pass the yf over the 2 sts knitted.

Note: On the first st of round and when changing needles, the easiest way to work the yf is to insert the right needle in the first stitch, bring the yarn under and then over that needle, then knit the stitch.

Method

This unisex pattern is worked using only one colour at a time. The glove starts at the wrist with rib, and the pattern is then worked for the hand, fingers and thumb. Both hands are worked the same, and there is an option to knit the fingers in plain stocking stitch. These gloves also look good worked in a single colour.

Glove

With 3mm needles and Tarn, cast on 48(52) sts and work in 2 x 2 rib for 2⅓(3)in [6(7.5)cm]. On the last row, inc as folls:

Woman's glove: (rib 6, M1) to end. 56 sts.

Man's glove: Rib 2, (rib 6, M1) to last 2 sts, rib 2. 60 sts.

Change to 3.5mm needles and k 1 row. Begin to work in patt as folls:

Pattern

Round 1: Using Heather, (yf, k2, psso) to end.

Round 2: Knit.

Rounds 3–4: Rep rounds 1–2 in Tarn. Twist the yarns round each another at the start of each round and pull to tighten up the join.

Cont in patt. *At the same time* start the thumb gusset on round 4 as folls:

Round 4: Patt 28(30), M2, patt to end. Place markers on each side of the M2.

Rounds 5–7: Patt across the k2 on the next 3 rounds.

Round 8: Within markers (M1R, k2, M1L).

Next 3 rounds: Within markers, (k1, patt 2, k1).

Cont in this way, *inc every other row* from now on and keeping patt correct by working (k1, patt over gusset sts, k1) every other inc as above until there are 18(18) sts for gusset.

Work until glove measures 2¾(3)in [7(7.5)cm] from start of patterning, ending on row 2 or 4 of patt.

Place the 18 gusset sts on a thread or safety pin. Cont in patt on 56(60) sts until work measures 3¾(4¼)in [9.5(11)cm] from start of patterning, ending on patt row 1 or 3. Break off yarn and place all but the first and last 6 sts on a thread. With thumb at the right, cont in patt.

Note: Some of the increases are unsymmetrical to keep the patt correct.

Fingers (woman's size)

Work first row (patt row 2 or 4):

Little finger

Cast on and k2 sts at the front, k6 sts from front needle, k6 sts from back needle, inc 2 sts as folls: (reverse work and cast on 2 sts, 16 sts.

Work in patt on these 16 sts for 2¼in (5.5cm), ending on a row 4 of patt.

Next round (top): (k2 tog) to end. Knit1 round, then break off yarn and pull end through to close.

Third (ring) finger

Next round: Inc 1, k7 sts on front needle, pick up 2 sts from base of previous finger, k7 sts on back needle, inc 1 (to keep patt correct). 18 sts.

Work for 2¼in (6.5cm), ending on a row 4 of patt.

* **Next 2 rounds:** (k2tog) to end. Break off yarn and pull end through to close *.

Second finger

Inc 2, k7 on front needle, pick up 2, k7 sts on back needle, inc 2. 20 sts.

Work for 2¾in (7cm) then work top as * to *.

Forefinger (first finger)

Pick up 4 from previous finger, knit across last 16 sts. 20 sts.

Work for 2½in (6.5cm) then as * to *.

Thumb (both sizes)

Using the same colour as the last row worked, pick up and k4 sts from the base of the thumb. Join in other colour. Work in patt for 2(2¼)in [5(5.5)cm], then work top as * to *.

Fingers (man's size)

Little finger

Inc 3, work 7 sts from front needle and 7 sts from back needle, inc 1. 18 sts. Work for 2½in (6.5cm), then work top as * to *.

Third (ring) finger

(7 sts from back and front).
Inc 2 at front, pick up 4 sts, inc 2 at end. 22 sts.
Work for 3in (7.5cm) then work top as * to *.

Second finger

(7 sts from back and front).
Inc 3, k7, pick up 4, k7, inc 1. 22 sts.
Work 3⅓in (8.5cm), then work top as * to *.

Forefinger (first finger)

Pick up 4 from base of second finger then knit across rem 18 sts. 22 sts. Work top as * to *.

Making up

Darn in ends. Lay under a damp cloth overnight.

Variation

Working the digits in pattern is fiddly but rewarding. If you find it too much, work in st st using Tarn as folls:

Woman's glove

Little finger: Inc 2, k6 from front and back. 14 sts.
Second and third fingers: Inc 2 sts, k7, pick up 2, k7. 18 sts.
Forefinger: Pick up 2 sts, k16. 18 sts.

Man's glove

Little finger: Inc 3 sts, k14. 17 sts.
Third finger: Inc 3 sts, k7, pick up 3, k7. 20 sts.
Second finger: Inc 3 sts, k7, pick up 3, k7. 20 sts.
Forefinger: Pick up 2, k18. 20 sts.

Rose pink and accessorized with pearly beads, these gloves couldn't be more girly. Topped with an elegant seam of cable knit, you'll want to be wearing these every time you go out.

Beaded beauty

Size

To fit woman

Circumference 7–8in (18–20cm) approx (the cable panel stretches to fit)

The length and fingers can be adjusted as required

Note: The sample was made to fit me and I have long fingers.

Average finger lengths are given on page 136, but it's best to measure

Tension

32 sts and 40 rows over 4in (10cm) over st st using 4mm needles

Bead and cable panel (exc. side purl sts) measures 1¼in (3cm) approx

Materials

Rowan pure wool 4ply 100% superwash wool (162m/174yds per 50g ball)

2 x 50g balls in 426 Hyacinth

A set of 3mm (UK11:US2–3) double-pointed needles

Cable needle

Beads (I used Gutermann Rocailles 9/0, or substitute any suitable bead – see Techniques, page 150)

Sewing needle and thread

Special abbreviations

C6f = Put next 3 sts on a CN and leave at front, knit next 3 sts, then knit sts from CN

C6b = Put next 3 sts onto CN and leave at back, knit next 3 sts, then knit sts from CN

Pb = Place bead

Method

This elegant glove is easier than it looks. It is worked from wrist to fingertips and the cabling at the back of the hands is complemented by beading.

Right glove

Thread beads on yarn (see page 150). Cast on 63 sts and set rib patt as folls (and on chart showing central patt):

Round 1: P2, k4, p2, k3, p3, panel, p3, k3, (p2, k4) 5 times.

Rounds 2, 6, 8, 10, 12, 14 and 16: Work as chart.

Round 3: P2, (C4f, p2), k3, p3, panel 13, p3, k3, (p2, C4b) 3 times, (p2, C4f) twice.

Round 4: Work cable panels as chart; knit across patt.

Round 5: Work as chart, pb for panel.

Rounds 7 and 15: Work cable panels and beads as chart.

Round 9 and 13: Place beads as chart.

Round 11: Cables and patt as chart.

Rep until rib measures 2½in (6.5cm). Move beg of the round 2 sts towards front so it begins k6, p3, panel, p3. Keeping central (p3, panel 13, p3) as set, work rem sts in st st. Cable panel and place beads as for chart. *At the same time* beg thumb on round 3 as folls: Work 36 sts, place marker, (M1R, k1, M1L), work 26 sts.

On every other round, k the gusset sts. Inc gusset by 2 sts (as above) on every third row, until it has 19 sts.

Work until 2¾in (7cm) or required length to thumb without further shaping. Place the 19 gusset sts on a thread and cont on 62 sts until work measures 3¾in (9.5cm) from rib, or desired length up to fingers.

Break off yarn. Place sts on a thread tied at the little finger end.

Little finger

Beg with palm facing, thumb at right, place 7 sts from front and 7 sts from back on dpns. Inc 3, k2, k2tog, work to end of round. 16 sts.

Work in st st for 2in (5cm) or to required length.

Next round (dec for top): (k2tog) to end of round.

Knit 1 more round, then break off yarn and pull end through sts to close *.

Note: If there is an odd st at the end of the round, end round k1.

Third (ring) finger

(8 sts from each end of thread). Inc 3, k3, k2tog, work rem 7 sts from front needle, pick up 3 sts from base of previous finger, k8. 21 sts.

Work for 2¾in (7cm) or desired length, the work top as for little finger.

Second finger

(8 sts from back and 7 sts from front of thread).

Inc 4, k4, k2tog, work 7 sts, pick up 3 sts, work 8 sts. 21 sts.

Work for 3in (7.5cm) then work top as for little finger.

Forefinger (first finger)

Place rem 17 sts on dpns, and pick up 3 sts. 20 sts.

Work for 2¾in (7cm) or desired length, then work top as for little finger.

Thumb

Take 19 sts from thread and pick up 3 from base of thumb. 22 sts.

Work for 1½in (4cm), or approx ¼in (6mm) less than desired length.

Next round: (k2tog, k1) to last 2 sts, k2tog. 14 sts.

Knit 1 round.

Next round: (k2tog) to end.

Next round: Knit.

Break off yarn and pull end through sts to close.

Beaded beauty *13 sts x 16 rows*

Each square = 1 st and 1 row

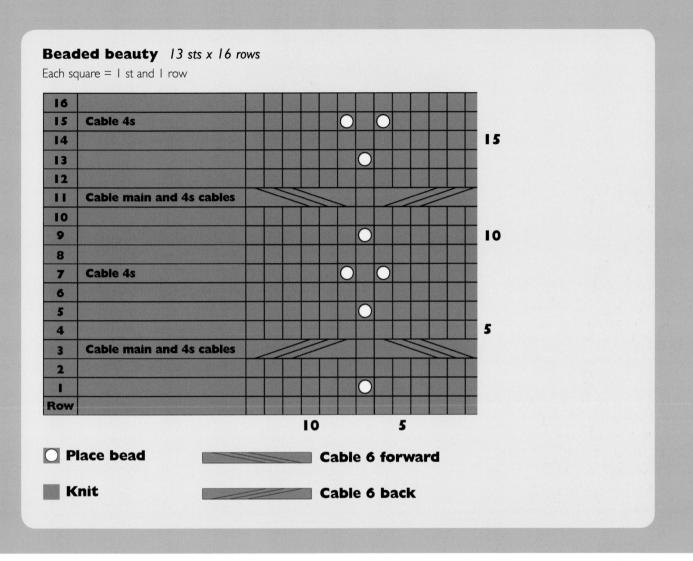

○ **Place bead**

■ **Knit**

Cable 6 forward

Cable 6 back

Left glove

Set pattern as folls: (k4, p2) 5 times, k3, p3, panel 13, p3, k3, (p2, k4), p2.

At end of rib move start of round back 4 sts (row on needles) so last row of rib is worked thus at new start of round: k2, p2, k4.

On round 3, set thumb as folls: K26, place marker, k1, place marker, k36. Cont as for right glove.

Making up

Darn in all ends and neaten any holes between fingers. Leave under a damp cloth overnight. Do not place a weight over cable.

Beautifully varied in colour, texture and pattern, these gloves will add an arty, multi-hued spark to your outfit. But take care – you may find yourself bombarded with pleas for Christmas presents!

Colorama

Size

To fit teen (woman:man)
Circumference 7(7½:8)in [19(20:18)cm]

Tension

24 sts and 38 rows to 4in (10cm) over slip st using 4mm needles

Materials

1 x 25g ball in 318 Woodgreen
1 x 25g ball in 286 Moorgrass
1 x 25g ball in 1260 Raspberry
1 x 25g ball in 1290 Loganberry
1 x 25g ball in 1270 Purple Haze
1 x 25g ball in 292 Pine Forest
1 x 25g ball in 272 Fog
A set of 4mm (UK8:US6) double-pointed needles
Note: Yarn requirements as for 'Moorland' (see page 112), apart from Mogit

Special abbreviations

T2 = Twist 2 sts (knit next 2 sts tog without removing them from needle, knit first st again, then slip both sts on to right needle)

S1 = Slip 1 st p-wise but keep yarn at back of work as if to knit

Pattern notes

Instructions for this glove are in three sizes: teen, man's and woman's. The design is the result of a time spent on a Greek island with no wool shop and only the yarn left over from 'Moorland' and 4mm needles. I love it, and it just proves that restricted materials can actually be liberating!

Slip stitch pattern

Round 1: (k2, s1) to end.
Round 2 and every alt round: Knit.
Round 3: (k1, s1,k1) to end
Round 5: (s1, k2) to end.
Note: The slipped stitch moves 1 st to the right with each colour change.

Colour sequence

Purple Haze
Loganberry
Fog
Woodgreen
Moorgrass
Pine Forest
Fog
Raspberry.

Method

This glove begins with a diagonal rib, then a simple slip stitch pattern for the hand, with only one colour worked at a time. The digits are in multiple colours.

Gloves

Using Raspberry, cast on 42(45:48) sts and join into a round to work rib.
Round 1: (k2, p1) to end.
Round 2: (T2, p1) to end.
Note: The rib forms diagonally. You can leave it like this, straighten it out at the finishing stage or use a (k3, p3) every row rib on 3.5mm or 3.25mm needles.
Rep rounds 1–2 for 2in (5cm).
Next round: Purl.
Next round: Knit.
Beg with Purple Haze and foll colour sequence, beg slip stitch patt for main section. *At the same time* work gusset, beg on round 4 and always working the incs on knit rounds, as folls:
Note: The woman's size has a left and a right glove. For man's and teen sizes both gloves are the same.
Woman's right glove: Work 24 sts, place marker, M1, place marker. Work 21 sts to end.
Woman's left glove: Work 21 sts, M1, work 24 sts to end.
Man's glove: Work 24 sts, M1, work 24 sts to end.
Teen glove: Work 21, M1, work 21 to end.

Cont in patt working gusset st as (k1) on even rows (the 'knit' row of patt) and taking them into patt when possible on the patt row as folls:
Round 8: Work to marker, (M1R, k1, M1L), work to end.
Rounds 9 and 11: Work patt across 3 gusset sts.
Round 12: Work to marker, (M1R, knit 3 gusset sts, M1L) work to end.
Round 13: Work to marker, (k1, patt 3, k1), work to end.
Round 14: Work to marker. (M1R, k5 M1L), work to end
Round 15: Work to marker, (k2, patt 3, k2), work to end.
Round 16: Work to marker (M1R, k7, M1L), work to end.
Round 17: Work to marker, patt across the 9 gusset sts.
Cont in this way, inc 2 sts every other row until the gusset has 15(19) sts. Work without further inc to 2½(3)in [6.5(7.5)cm] from rib ending on a patt row. Work gusset sts, slip them on to a holder or thread, patt to end of round. Cont to work in patt on the rem 45 sts until work measures 3¾in (9.5cm) or required length, ending with a k row. Work 1 round purl.
Break off yarn and place all sts on waste yarn or stitch holders.
Fingers are worked with thumb on right, beg at little finger end.

Little finger

Using Woodgreen, place 5 sts from back and 5 sts from front on 4mm dpns. Inc 2(3) sts at thumb end. Knit these 2 sts and 5 sts from front, then nit 5 sts from back. 12(12:13) sts. Work 2(2¼:2½)in [5(5.5:6.5)cm].

Work top: ** (k2tog) across round, ending (k3tog) if there are an odd number of sts.

Note: If you have smaller needles use them for these rows.

Knit 1 round.

Break off yarn and pull end through to close **.

Third (ring) finger

Using Loganberry, take 5(5:6) sts from the front and 5(6:6) sts from the back. Inc 2 sts and k them, k5(5:6) sts from front needle. Pick up 2 sts from base of little finger, knit back needle sts. 14(15:16) sts.

Work for 2¼(2½:3)in [5.5(6.5:7.5)cm]. Work top as ** to **.

Second finger

Using Moorgrass, take 5(6:6) sts from the front and 5(5:6) sts from the back. Inc 2 sts and knit them, k5(5:6) sts from front needle. Pick up 2 sts from base of third finger, knit back needle sts. 14(15:16) sts.

Work for 2½ (2¾:3⅓)in [6.5(7:8.5)cm]. Work top as ** to **.

Forefinger (first finger)

Using Purple Haze place rem 12(13:15) sts on dpns. Pick up 2 sts from base of third finger and knit them, knit across back then front sts. 14(15:16) sts. Work length and top as for third finger.

Thumb

Using Raspberry, place 15(19) thumb sts on dpns. Pick up 1 st at base of thumb. 18(20) sts.

Work 2 rounds st st..

Next round: Knit to last 3 sts, (sl1, k2tog, psso). 16(18) sts.

Work until thumb measures 1½in (4cm).

Next round: (k2tog, k1) across round, ending round k3tog). 11(12) sts.

Next round: Knit.

Next round: (k2tog) to last 3 sts, k3tog. 5(6) sts

Next round: Knit.

Break off yarn and pull end through to close.

Making up

Darn in ends. Pin rib straight if desired. Leave overnight under damp cloth with polythene and a heavy book or similar weight on top.

Dazzlingly bright, these mittens will brighten up even the darkest winter day – although you may find that you attract more attention than you bargained for!

Dyed in the wool

Size
Child
To fit 6–10years (10years–teen)
Circumference 6½(7)in [16(18)cm]
Length wrist to fingers 3(3⅓)in [7.5(8.5)cm]
Total length 7(8¼)in [18(21)cm]

Adult
To fit average woman
Circumference 7½in (19cm)
Length (wrist to fingers) 3¾in (9.5cm) or as desired
Total length 9½in (24cm) or as desired

Tension
21 sts and 26 rows to 4in (10cm) over st st using
4.5mm needles
Use larger or smaller needles to achieve correct tension

Materials
Uppingham's Pura Lana Ecologica 100% ecological wool
(85m/92yds per 50g ball)
2 x 50g in 80 Cream (example has been dyed – see
Techniques, page 151)
A set each 3.75mm (UK9:US5) and 4.5mm (UK7:US7)
double-pointed needles

Method

These matching flip-tops are perfect for mother and child. Colouring the yarn is an ideal half-term or holiday activity, or leave it undyed if you prefer. Food products are used for the dyeing (see page 151), so it is perfectly safe, and a microwave is used to lessen the risk of burns.

Child's mittens

Note: The adult version has separate fingers beneath the flip-top, but a mitten is easier for children to manage.

With 3.75mm needles cast on 36(40) sts and work in 2 x 2 rib for 2⅓in (6cm), dec 1 st on the last row. 35(39) sts.

Change to 4.75mm needles and proceed in st st, beg thumb gusset as folls on round 3.

Right hand: Work 18(20) sts, M1R, k1, M1L, work 16(18) to end of round.

Left hand: Work 16(18), sts, M1R, k1, M1L, work 18(20) to end of round.

Cont in st st, work gusset incs on every other row until there are 11(13) sts. Work until gusset is 2¼(2⅓)in [5.5(6cm] or required length from wrist. Place gusset sts on a safety pin or waste yarn and cont on 34(38) sts until work measures 3¼(3½)in [8(9)cm] from rib or desired length to base of fingers.

Change to 3.75mm needles and rib 5 rows.

Cast off in rib.

Thumb

Place 11(13) gusset sts from pin on dpns and inc 2 sts from base of thumb. 13(15) sts.

Work in the round for 1½(1¾)in [3.75(4.5)cm] or desired thumb length. Using smaller needles (k2tog) to last st, k1. 6(7) sts.

Knit 1 round.

Break off yarn and pull end through sts to close.

See below for flip-top.

Adult size

With 3.75mm dpns cast on 44 sts and work in 2 x 2 rib in the round for 2½in (6.5cm). On the last round dec by (k2tog, k12) to last 2sts, k2. 41 sts.

Change to 4.5mm needles.

Cont in st st. *At the same time* on the third round begin thumb:

Right thumb: Work 23 sts, place marker, M1R, k1, M1L, place marker, work to end.

Left thumb: Work 17, place marker, work 23 sts, work to end.

Rounds 4–6 (either glove): Knit.
Round 7 (either glove): Work to gusset, M1R, k3, M1L, work to end. Cont in this way, inc for gusset on rounds 10, 13, 16, 18, and 20 (15 sts in gusset).
Next round: Knit.

Place gusset sts on waste yarn.

Next round: Inc 2 sts above gusset by inc into last st before gusset as well as into the foll st. 42 sts.

Cont on these sts until work measures 3¾in (9.5cm) from wrist or desired measurement.

Break off yarn and place sts, apart from 5 sts at each side of yarn, on waste yarn tied at little finger end. These are the little finger sts (with thumb at right).

Little finger

Using 3.75 needles, inc 2 sts, then (p2, k2) across sts to end. 12 sts.

Work 5 rounds in st st.

Cast off loosely in rib

Third and second fingers

Place 5 sts from each end of waste yarn on a dpn. Inc 3 sts and, beg p2, work 2 x 2 rib across sts on first needle, pick up 3 sts and cont rib across sts on back needle. 16 sts.

Work 5 rows st st.

Cast off in rib.

Forefinger (first finger)

Place rem 12 sts on dpns. Pick up 4 sts, p1, k2, p1, then cont in 2 x 2 rib to end. 16 sts.

Work 5 rows st st.

Cast off in rib.

Thumb

Place sts from waste yarn on dpns, inc 3 sts at base. 18 sts.

Work 2 rounds, then on third round knit last st of row tog with first st of next round, k1, skpo. 16 sts.

Work for 1½in (4cm).

Next row: K2, (k2tog) to end. 12 sts.

Work 2 rows.

Using smaller needles, (k2tog) to end.

Knit 1 row and pull yarn through.

Darn in as many ends as possible before beg to work flip-top.

Flip-top
(children's sizes in brackets)

NB see Techniques, page 147.

Pick up 21(18:20) sts from back of mitten and leave on one side.

Cast on 20(18:20) sts. Working back and forth on 4.5mm needles, work 2 rows g-st then with 3.75mm needles work 4 rows 2 x 2 rib.

Change to 4.75mm dpns and work 1 row across these sts. Join to the picked-up back sts.

Adult size only: Knit tog the last st of the cast-on and the first st of the back. 40 sts.

Note: If you require the top a little looser do not work this dec; cast on 1 st at beg of next round instead. 42 sts.

Rearrange sts over 3 dpns. Children's sizes have 36(40) sts.

Cont in st st until work measures 8(6½:6¾)in [20(16:17.5)cm] from start.

Note: This will produce a finished mitten measuring approx 9½(7¾:8½)in [24(20:21.5)cm] from start. Work a few extra rounds at this point if you want more length.

Place marker at start and halfway mark of yarn (20 sts each side).

Next round (dec for top): (k2tog tbl, work to 2 sts before marker, k2tog). Rep instructions in bracket once. 16 sts.

Next round: Knit.

Cont in this way, dec on every other row until 24(18:20) sts rem, ending with a knit row. Divide sts 12(9:10) on each needle and cast off using the 3-needle method (see page 139).

Left flip-top

Pick up back sts and leave as above.

Work the rows of g-st and rib as before and break off yarn. Set aside.

Return to the picked-up stitches across the back. Beg from thumb end, attach yarn, knit across back picked-up sts then across the rib sts on the put-aside needle beg from broken-off yarn end. Form into a ring round the fingers and purl the round, joining first and last sts. 40(36:40) sts.

Note: On both gloves, the round starts at the thumb end but on the right glove it goes across the front rib sts first. On the left glove it goes over the back picked-up sts first.

Work rest of top as for right flip-top.

Making up

Darn in rem ends. Leave under a wet cloth overnight. Place a polythene bag over the damp cloth and place a book or similar weight on top.

Sailor-style in striped cream and navy, these gloves are perfect for both male and female seafarers. Bold and beautiful, your hands certainly won't get cold as you contemplate ocean voyages!

Matelot

Size

To fit S(M:L)

Circumference 6½(7¼:8)in [16.5(18.5:20)cm]

Small size fits from approx 10 years to petite woman

Medium size fits average woman

Large size fits large woman or average man

Tension

24 sts and 30 rows to 4in (10cm) over st st using 4mm needles

Use larger or smaller needles to achieve correct tension

Materials

Cygnet Superwash DK 100% pure new wool (104m/114yds per 50g ball)

1 x 50g ball in 2195 Cream

1 x 50g bell in 0298 Cranberry

1 x 50g ball in 2153 Navy

A set each 3.5mm (UK9–10:US4) and 4mm (UK8:US6) needles

Safety pin and waste yarn for holding stitches

Pattern notes

Striped st st patt

Round 1: Using Navy, knit.

Rounds 2–4: Using Cream, knit.

Rep these four rounds for stripe patt.

Method

These gloves with a nautical theme are made in pure wool. The 2 x 2 rib at the wrist is worked in Cranberry and Navy, and a 4-round stripe pattern repeat in Cream and Navy is used for the hand. Fingers and thumb are worked in Navy.

Right glove

Using 3.5mm needles and Cranberry, cast on 40(44:48) sts and work 2 rounds in 2 x 2 rib.

Change to Navy and cont in 2 x 2 rib for 2(2⅓:2¾)in [5(6:7)cm].

Change to 4mm needles and beg striped st st patt, rep rounds 1–4 throughout hand.

Note: To disguise join at start of the stripe round, knit the first st of the next round in Navy. At the same time, beg on round 5, work thumb gusset: K23(25:27) sts, M1. Place marker each side of M1, knit to end. 17(19:21) sts.

Next round: Knit all sts (inc the M1).

Round 7: Work to marker; (M1R, k1, M1L), work to end.

Inc 2 sts in this way on alternate rows, knitting the newly made stitches on foll rows, until gusset has 15(15:17) sts.

Cont until work measures 2½(2¾:3)in [6.5(7:7.5)cm] from beg. Place thumb sts on a safety pin or thread.

Cont until hand measures 3⅓(3¾:4¼)in [8.5(9.5:10.5)cm] or desired length. Break off yarn. Place all sts on waste yarn tied at the little finger end, thumb to right and palm uppermost. Divide for fingers by taking sts from back and front of waste yarn as folls:

Little finger

Inc 2 sts and knit them, work 10(12:14) sts from back and front threads. Join into a round. Work for 2(2¼:2⅓)in [5(5.5:6)cm] or desired length.

Next round: * Change to 3.5mm needles and (k2tog) to end.

Next round: Knit to end.

Break off yarn and pull end through sts to close *.

Third (ring) finger

Inc 2 sts and knit them, k5 sts, pick up 2 sts from base of little finger, k5, join these sts into a round. 14 sts.

Work to 2¼(2½:2¾)in [5.5(6.5:7)cm].

Work top as * to *.

Second finger

Inc 2 sts and knit them, k5(5:6), pick up 2 sts from base of third finger, k5(5:6), join sts into a round. 14(14:16) sts.

Work to 2½(2¾:3)in [6.5(7:7.5)cm] or desired length. Work top as * to *.

Forefinger (first finger)

Pick up 2 sts from base of third finger and knit them, k12(14:14) sts. Form these 14(16:16) sts into a round and work for 2¼(2½:2¾)in [5.5(6.5:7)cm] or desired length. Work top as * to *.

Average finger measurements

Size	Little finger	Third finger	Second finger	First finger
Small	1½in (4cm)	2in (5cm)	2in (5cm)	2⅓ in (6cm)
Medium	2in (5cm)	2in (5cm)	2in (5cm)	2¾ in (7cm)
Large	2⅓ in (6cm)	2in (5cm)	2⅓ in (6cm)	2¾ in (7cm)

Thumb

Return to sts on pin or thread. Pick
up 2 sts at base of thumb and knit
them, work across 13(15:17) thumb
sts. 15(17:19)sts.

Work in patt for 1½(1¾:2)in
[4(4.5:5)cm].

Change to 3.5mm needles and work
top k1, (k2tog) to last 0(2:1) sts,
(k2tog, k1) 10(11:13) sts.

Next round: (k2tog) to end (last
3: last 3) sts, k0(k3tog: k3tog).
5(5:6) sts.

Break off yarn and pull end through
sts to close.

Left glove

Work as for right hand until setting
of gusset, then place gusset as folls:
K17(19:21), M1, then knit rem
23(25:27) sts. Proceed as for right
glove to fingers. Pick up fingers with
thumb at the right, back uppermost.

Making up

Darn in all ends, and neaten fingers.
Place damp cloth over gloves and
leave overnight.

These gloves create a smooth blend of moorland beauty: the wild flowers, the greenery and the unpredictable terrain. But beware that you don't attract the local wildlife.

Moorland

Size

To fit man
Circumference 8¾in (22cm)
Wrist to fingers 4¾in (12cm)

Tension

Approx 25 sts to 4in (10cm) over Fairisle using 4.5mm needles
Main pattern rep: approx 14 sts to 2¼in (5.5cm), and approx 14 rows to 2⅓in (6cm)
Fingers: 26 sts and 34 rows to 4in (10cm) using 4mm needles
Use larger or smaller needles to achieve correct tension

Materials and equipment

Jamieson's Shetland DK 100% wool (75m/82yds per 25g ball)
1 x 25g ball in 107 Mogit or Sand 183
1 x 25g ball in 318 Woodgreen
1 x 25g ball in 286 Moorgrass
1 x 25g ball in 1260 Raspberry (used for one row only)
1 x 25g ball in 1290 Loganberry
1 x 25g ball in 1270 Purple Haze
1 x 25g ball in 292 Pine Forest
1 x 25g ball in 272 Fog
A set each of 3.25mm (UK10:US3), 4mm (UK8:US6) and 4.5mm (UK7:US7) double-pointed needles

Tip

The Shetland rib is not very stretchy. If you prefer a stretchier rib use a 2 x 2 rib in a single colour.

Pattern notes

This handsome man's glove in Shetland DK uses traditional Shetland patterns but in a slightly thicker yarn than usual. *Note: I had enough of these colours to knit both this glove and 'Colorama' (see page 100). There was only just enough Mogit left for the fingers, so you might like to order an extra ball. If you want to knit the fingers of 'Colorama' all in one colour, add 1 ball.*

Method

Work in the round beg at wrist, patterning in bands of Fairisle and finishing with the fingers and thumb.

Gloves

With 3.25mm needles cast on 52 sts in Fog and work in the round.

Round 1: (k2 Fog, p2 Pine) to end. Rep for 2⅓in (6cm).

On last round (keeping rib as correct as possible), inc 4 as folls: (work 13, M1) 4 times. 56 sts.

Change to 4.5mm needles.

Work 1 round Fog.

Work 1 round Mogit.

Pattern 1

Work Chart 1 (patt rep = 7 sts x 5 rows).

Work 1 round Mogit.

This forms the first pattern band.

Work 1 round Woodgreen.

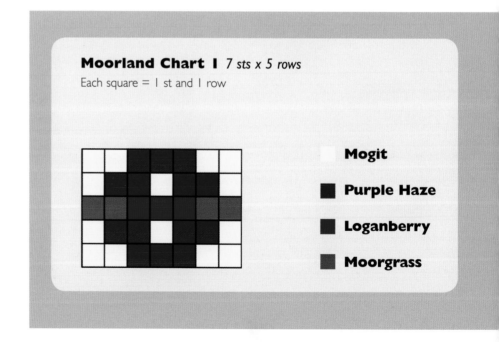

Moorland Chart 1 *7 sts x 5 rows*

Each square = 1 st and 1 row

☐ **Mogit**

■ **Purple Haze**

■ **Loganberry**

■ **Moorgrass**

Pattern 2

Work Chart 2 (patt rep = 14 sts x 15 rows) to form second pattern band. Work 1 round Woodgreen.

At the same time on round 12 or when wrist to thumb measures 3in (7.5cm) or desired length work thumb:

Left hand

Work 22 sts, work the next 8 sts and slide them back on left needle. Work these 8 sts only again using waste yarn, then cont in patt to end of round.

Right hand

Work 27 sts, work the next 8 sts and slide back on left needle. Work with contrast yarn as left hand.

Both hands

On the next row just work in patt over the contrast sts.

Note: If you want to try the glove on to check the position of the thumb and the finger length, work several rows in contrast yarn, then cut it across the middle. This will allow you to get a thumb through, but take care that it doesn't unravel. Another way to check measurements is to cast off the 8 thumb sts, then cast them on again on the following row – but this method will produce a less flexible thumb opening.

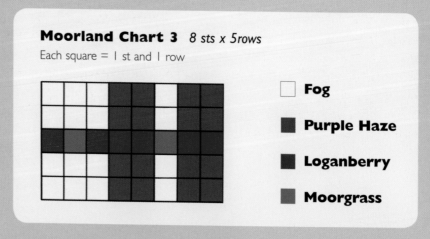

Moorland Chart 2 *14 sts x 15 rows*
Each square = 1 st and 1 row

Thumb row

- Woodgreen
- Pine Forest
- Moorgrass
- Purple Haze
- Loganberry
- Raspberry

Moorland Chart 3 *8 sts x 5 rows*
Each square = 1 st and 1 row

- Fog
- Purple Haze
- Loganberry
- Moorgrass

Pattern 3

Work 1 round Fog, then work Chart 3 (patt rep = 8 sts x 5 rows). Work 1 round Fog, then 1 round Mogit on 4mm needles ready to work fingers.

Fingers

Put all sts on stitchholders, or waste yarn tied at little-finger end, and break off yarn. Work in Mogit on 4mm needles. With thumb to the right work fingers as follows:

Little finger

* Place 7 sts from front and back on dpns *, inc1. 15 sts.
Work in the round for 2½in (6.5cm) or desired length.
Change to 3.25 needles, (k2tog) to last 3 sts, k3tog.
Next round: Knit.
Break off yarn and pull end through sts to close.

Third (ring) finger

Inc 2 sts at beg of round and knit them, k7 sts, pick up 2 sts from base of last finger, k7. 18 sts.
Next round: Knit.
Round 3: K2tog, k7, skpo, k7 (so the 2 fourchette sts are reduced to 1). 16 sts.

Work 3in (7.5cm) or desired length.
** Work top: Change to 3.25 needles, (k2tog) to the last 3 sts, k3tog.
Next round: Knit.
Break off yarn and pull end through sts to close **.

Second finger

As for third finger but work to 3⅓in (8.5cm).

Forefinger (first finger)

As * to *, then pick up 2 sts from base of second finger. 16 sts.
Work for 3in (7.5cm) then ** to ** for top.

Right thumb

Pick up 8 sts from top and bottom of waste yarn. Beg from side of glove, using 4.5mm needles and Woodgreen, pick up 2 sts bet the 2 rows of picked-up sts. Patt across front of thumb, pick up 3 sts from the other side of the thumb opening. Knit 8 sts across back of thumb, leaving a long end to work next 2 Fairisle rows at front only.
Note: Do not carry Pine Forest round as it will restrict flexibility of the glove.
Complete Fairisle rows at front only, to match star patt on rounds 13–15.

Change to 4mm needles and Mogit. and work until thumb measures 2in (5cm) or about ¼in (.5cm) less than desired finished length. Dec 1 st at the palm side of the thumb gusset on the last Woodgreen row. 20 sts.
Next round: (k2tog) to end. 10 sts.
Next round: Change to 3.25 needles. (k2tog) to end. 5 sts.
Break off yarn and pull end through sts to close.

Making up

Shetland can be washed and stretched into shape. The Shetlanders use glove boards but damping the gloves and placing a damp towel, polythene and a book on top seems to work well.

Inspired by bold and daring traditional patterns, these striking gloves
feature a sophisticated symmetrical design.
A timeless classic.

Nordic squares

Size

To fit 10 years–teen (woman:man)
Circumference approx 7(7½:8¼)in [18(19:21)cm]

Tension

25 sts and 30 rows to 4in (10cm) over patt using
4mm needles
Use larger or smaller needles to achieve correct tension

Materials

Pura Lana Ecologica Aran 100% ecological wool
(85m/93yds per 50g ball)
1 × 50g ball in 154 Charcoal (MC)
1 × 50g ball in 53 Mushroom (CC)
A set each 3.5mm (UK9–10:US4) and 4mm (UK8:US6)
needles

Special abbreviations

S1 = Slip 1 st p-wise but keep yarn on knit side.

Pattern notes

I thought of this as a male pattern but it really is unisex. The inspiration came from simple Scandinavian and Shetland designs.

Method

There are two pattern variations: choose between Fairisle (which is faster but uses 2 colours in a row) and slip stitch versions. Each pattern is written in rows for clarity. Both gloves are worked the same, starting with rib at the wrist, working in pattern over the hand, then completing the fingers and thumb. Take care not to pull the yarns too tightly across the back of the work.

Gloves

Using 3.5mm needles and MC, cast on 44(48:52) sts and work in 2 x 2 rib.
Round 1: (k2, p2) to end.
Rounds 2–6(8:8): Rep row 1.
Change to CC and work 2 more rounds in rib.
Work 2 rounds rib in MC, 2 rounds rib in CC, then 6(8:8) rounds in MC.
Change to 4mm needles and work hand, using either patt method, as folls:

Fairisle pattern (over 5 rows)

Rows 1–3: Knit using MC.
Rows 4–5: (k1MC, k2CC, k1MC) to end of row. (4-st patt rep)
Rep rows 1–5 for hand patt.

Slip stitch pattern (over 7 rows)

Rows 1–3: Knit using MC.
Rows 4 and 4A: (both the same) Using CC only (s1MC, k2CC, s1MC), rep to end of row.
Rows 5 and 5B: (both the same) Using MC only (k1, s2, k1) to end.
Note: The CC from 2 rows previously are slipped, and the slipped sts are knitted.
This method produces exactly the same pattern effect as the Fairisle method, but is worked over 7 rows rather than 5 rows. Rep these 7 rows for hand patt.
At the same time beg gusset on round 3 (MC) setting patt outside as folls:
Work 22(24:26) sts, place marker, M2, place marker, knit to end.
Next round: (Patt row 4) Work up to marker as folls:

Fairisle method

First and third sizes: (k1MC, k2CC, k1MC) 5 times, k1CC (marker) knit in MC across gusset (marker) k1CC, (k1MC, k2CC, k1MC) 5 times to end of round.
Second size: (k1MC, k2CC, k1MC) 6 times to gusset, knit in MC across gusset, (k1MC, k2CC, k1MC) 6 times to end of round.
Rep for row 5.

Slip stitch rounds 4 and 4A

First and third sizes: (sp1MC, k2CC, sp1MC) 5 times, sp1MC, k1, work in CC to gusset, sp1 across gusset, k1CC, sp1MC, (sp1MC, k2CC, sp1MC) 5 times to end.
Second size: (sp1MC, k2CC, sp1MC) 6 times to gusset, sp1 across gusset, (sp1MC, k2CC, sp1MC) 6 times to end.
Rep for row 4A.

Rounds 5 and 5A

First and third sizes: (k1MC, sp2CC, k1MC) 5 times, (k1, sp1) in CC to gusset, k1MC across gusset, sp1CC, k1MC, (k1MC, sp2CC, k1MC) 5 times to end.
Second size: (sp1MC, sp2CC, k1MC).
Note: Patt rows outside the gusset will now rem as set for the whole hand.
Cont to inc gusset on the foll MC knit rounds, inc 2 sts each time using M1R at first marker and M1L at second.

Use a MC loop from below (in some cases more than 1 row below) for the M inc.

Round 6: (4 sts after inc) knit gusset sts in patt rows in MC.

Round 8: (6 sts after inc) work gusset bet markers in patt rows 9 and 10 and 9A and 10A to show as (2MC, 2CC, 2MC).

Round 11: (8 sts after inc) work gusset sts in patt rows in MC.

Round 13: (10 sts after inc) work gusset sts in patt rows in MC.

Rounds 14 and 14A: Work gusset sts in patt rows to show (2CC, 2MC) twice, 2CC.

Rounds 15 and 15A: Work gusset sts in patt rows to show (2CC, 2MC) twice, 2CC. 10 sts.

Round 16: (12 sts after inc) work gusset sts in patt rows in MC.

Round 18: (14 sts after inc) work gusset sts in patt rows in MC.

Round 19: Work gusset sts in patt to show (2MC, 2CC) 3 times, 2MC. 14 sts.

Cont without further incs for first size and with 1 further inc for second and third sizes until hand section measures 2½(2¾:3)in [6.5(7:7.5)cm] from rib (or desired length), ending on a MC round. Knit the gusset sts and place on a holder or thread.

Cont in patt until work measures 3⅓(3¾:4¼)in [8.5(9.5:10.5)cm] to fingers, finishing on a MC round. Break off yarn and place all sts on holders or thread.

Now work fingers using Charcoal.

Little finger

Place 5(5:6) sts from back and front of glove on dpns. Inc 2 sts and knit them, then work sts from front and back. 12(12:14) sts.

Work for 2(2¼ : 2½) [5(5.5:6.5)cm].

Next round (work top): Using 3.5mm needles, ** (k2tog) to end.

Note: If round ends with an odd number of sts, k3tog at the end.

Knit 1 round.

Break off yarn and pull end through sts to close **.

Third (ring) finger

Place 5(6:7) sts from back and 6 sts from front on dpns. Inc 2 sts and knit them, knit sts from front, pick up 2 sts from base of previous finger, knit sts from back. 15(16:17) sts.

Work for 2¼(2½:3)in [5.5(6.5:7.5)cm], then work top as ** to **.

Second finger

Take 6 sts from back and 5(6:7) from front. Work as for third finger for 2½(2¾:3⅓)in [6.5(7:8.5)cm], then work top as ** to **.

Forefinger (first finger)

Place rem 12(14:14) sts on dpns. Pick up 2 sts from base of previous finger. 14(16:16) sts.

Work to same length as third finger, then work top as ** to **.

Thumb

Place 14(16:16) gusset sts on dpns. Pick up 2(2:2) sts at base of thumb and work for 1½(2:2¼)in [4(5:5.5)cm], then work top as ** to **.

Making up

Darn in all ends and leave under a damp cloth overnight.

The lurid green, craftily textured rectangles form a cosy setting of pastures, on which these joyful sheep laze. These fun gloves will cheer you up as soon as you put them on.

Grazing sheep

Size

To fit S[L]

Circumference 6⅓ –7(7–8)in [16–18(18–20)cm] approx (stretchy)

Smaller size fits 8years–teenage

Larger size fits average–large adult

You may need to adjust the finger lengths

Tension

24 sts and 33 rows to 4in (10cm) over patt using 4mm needles

Use larger or smaller needles to achieve correct tension

Materials

Debbie Bliss Cashmerino DK 55% merino wool 33% microfibre 12% cashmere (110m/120yds per 50g ball)

2 x 50g balls in 011 Green

A set each 3.25mm (UK10:US3) and 4mm (UK8:US6) double-pointed needles

6 sheep buttons

Method

This glove begins with an unusual (k1, p1) rib at the wrist, then a chequerboard-style textured pattern which combines a (k4, p2) rib with horizontal bands of garter stitch. The fingers and thumb are then completed in stocking stitch. Finally, cute sheep buttons are sewn on as decoration.

Right glove

Cast on 42(48) sts with 3.25mm needles.

Working in the round, work the rib as folls: (k1, p2) to end.

Cont in rib for 2⅓in (6cm).

Change to 4mm needles.

Rounds 1–7(8): K4, p2) to end.

Round 8(9): (P4, k4) to end

Round 9(10): As rounds 1–7.

Round 10(11): (P4, k2) to end.

Rounds 11–18(12–19): As rounds 1–7.

Round 19(20): As round 8.

Round 20(21): As round 10.

Rounds 21–28(22–29): As rounds 1–7.

Row 29(30): As round 8(9).

Round 30(31): As round 10(11).

Rep rows 21–28 until work measures 3⅓(3½)in [8.5(9)cm] or desired length to fingers. *At the same time work gusset*

On round 3: Work 23(26), M1, work 19(22).

On round 6: Work 23(26), (M1R, k1, M1L), work 19(22).

On round 9: Work 23(26), (M1R, k3, M1L), work 19(22).

Cont in this way knitting the gusset sts on every row and increasing 2 sts as above every other row until there are 15 gusset sts.

Cont working until piece measures 2½(2¾)in [6.5(7)cm] or desired length to top of thumb gusset.

Work next row and put gusset sts onto a thread.

Cont in patt until work measures 3½(3¾)in [9(9.5)cm] or desired length to fingers.

Break off yarn and put sts onto a thread with ends tied at little finger end (start of round).

Work fingers (thumb at right).

Little finger

Take 5(5) sts from front and back of glove (5 from each end of thread). Inc 2, k10.

Work in the round on these 12 sts for 1¾(2¼)in [4.5(5.5)cm].

Work top: * Change to 3.25mm needles, (K2tog) to end.

K 1 row.

Break off yarn and pull end though sts to close *.

Second and third fingers

Take next 5(6) sts from each side of thread. Inc 2, work 5, pick up 2 from base of last finger.

Work 2¼(2⅓)in [5.5(6)cm] on these sts for the third finger and 2⅓(2½)in [6(6.5)cm] for the second finger, working top as * to *.

Forefinger (first finger)

Pick up 2 sts from base of previous finger and work rem 12 sts.

Work 2¼(2⅓)in [5.5(6)cm] on these 14 sts and then top as * to *.

Thumb

Put 15 gusset sts onto needles. Pick up 1 st at base of thumb and work for 1½(2)in [4(5)cm]. Then work top as * to *.

Left hand

Small size only: The rib is worked (P2, k1) to end and the main patt starts (p2, k4). To set the gusset on row 3, (work 19, M1, work 23). Inc gusset on the same rows as the right hand.

Large size only: Work as for right hand but set gusset as folls: Work 26, M1, work 22. Inc gusset on the same rows as the right hand.

Making up

Sew in ends. Leave under a damp cloth overnight. Sew on buttons as in picture or as desired.

These stylish gloves are straightforward to make and warm both in heat and colour. They're what you call functional fashion, with their chic hint of tweed and finger freedom.

Tweed toastie

Size

Circumference approx 7½in (19cm)

These gloves are very stretchy

Tension

25 sts and 35 rows to 4in (10cm) over patt using 4mm needles

Use larger or smaller needles to achieve correct tension

Materials

Rowan Felted Tweed 50% merino wool 25% alpaca 25% viscose/rayon (175m/190yds per 50g ball)

1 x 50g ball in 160 Gilt

A set each 3mm (UK11:US2-3) and 4mm UK8:US6) double-pointed needles

Safety pin (for thumb stitches)

Pattern notes

The same stitch pattern was used throughout. If you prefer a snugger cuff and top, use a 3 x 3 rib (i.e. row 2 of patt only) and substitute 3.25mm dpns for the 3mm needles.

Method

Begin at the wrist and cast on using 4mm needles, then change to 3mm needles and work in 3 x 3 rib/garter stitch combination for the cuff. Change to 4mm needles again and cont in patt, inc for thumb gusset as you work. Change to 3mm needles for top of hand, and finish off thumb to match.

Handwarmers

Cast on 48 sts using 4mm needles, then change to 3mm needles for cuff:
* Knit 1 round.
Purl 1 round.
Still using 3mm needles, work in patt:
Row 1: Knit.
Row 2: (k3, p3) to end.
Rep these 2 rows for patt, noting that odd rows are knit rows and even rows are 3x3 rib rows *.
Work cuff for 2¾in (7cm) ending with a rib row (a row 2).

Change to 4mm needles and cont in patt for 2 rounds. On round 3 (a knit row of patt) set the gusset as folls:
Right hand: Work 27 sts, place marker, M1, place marker, work 24 sts.
Left hand: Work 24 sts, place marker, M1, place marker, work 27 sts.
Work a further 3 rows in patt, knitting the gusset st.
Round 7: Work to first gusset marker, (M1R, k1, M1L), work to end.
Note: The gusset itself is symmetrical, but there are 3 knit sts before it and 3 purl sts after it.
Patt 3 more rows, knitting the 3 gusset sts. This is the central pattern block of the gusset.
Round 11: Work to marker, (M1R, k3, M1L), work to end.
Next round: Patt to marker, (p1, k3, p1), patt to end.
Cont adding to the gusset in this way on every alt row, working the extra sts into the patt from now on until the gusset has 15 sts.
Round 22: (k3, p3, k3, p3, k3).
Round 23: Work to marker, (M1R, work 15, M1L). 17 gusset sts.
Round 24: Work to marker, p1, (k3, p3) twice, k3, p1.

Round 25: (Knit round) Place gusset sts on a safety pin for thumb. This should be about 5¾in (14.5cm) from start.
Adjust length here if necessary.
Cont in patt on 48 sts until work measures 6⅔in (17cm) approx or desired length to base of fingers, ending with a rib row.
Change to 3mm needles for top.
Work * to * as for cuff for ¾in (2cm) ending with a rib row.
Knit 1 round.
Purl 1 round.
Cast off using 4mm needles.

Thumb

Place the 17 thumb sts on 3mm dpns, inc 1 st at base of thumb. 18 sts.
Work in patt as for top of handwarmer for ¾in (2cm).
Cast off using 4mm needles.

Making up

Darn in ends and leave overnight under a damp cloth.

This graceful glove evokes the feel of the Victorian age in its pale tone and delicate patterning. Think long dresses, four-poster beds and dashing young suitors – you may just get swept off your feet!

Victoriana gloves

Size

To fit S/M woman (see pattern notes for M/L size)
Circumference 7in (18cm) approx
Length from wrist to hand 3½in (9cm) (adjustable)
Finger lengths adjustable

Tension

27 sts and 46 rows to 4in (10cm) over main body pattern using 3mm needles
Use larger or smaller needles to achieve correct tension

Materials Twilley's Lyscordet 3ply 100% mercerised cotton (200m/220yds per 50g ball)
1 x 50g ball in 21 Ecru
A set of 3mm (UK11:US2–3) needles
Corded elastic (use shirring elastic doubled, or a single strand of slightly stronger rounded cord)
Safety pin and waste yarn

Pattern notes

Because this pattern stretches in both directions it will fit most hands but you will need to adjust the length (i.e. the more it stretches widthwise, the more rows you will need for the length). For the M/L size, you will need to add about ¼–½in (6–12mm) to the finger lengths.

Method

Victoriana is a lace glove, knitted in the round on 4 needles in 3-ply cotton. Begin with a frill at the wrist and continue with the hand. Work fingers using the lace patt used for the frill, or for a fingerless glove, stop here and elasticate the top of the hand. The thumb is worked last.

Glove

Cast on 96 sts for frill and divide between 3 needles (30+30+36 sts). *Note: As this is a diagonal pattern it helps if all 6 rep sts are the same needle. This is also the case when working the fingers, which are in the same pattern.* Work 2 rounds g-st (knit 1 round, purl 1 round) for edge, then begin patt.

Pattern

Row 1: (k2tog, k2tog, yf, k1, yf, k1) to end.
Row 2: Knit.
Work approx 1¼in (3cm) in patt for frill, ending after a row 1.
Next round: (k2tog) to end, weaving in the doubled shirring elastic (or single cord elastic) on every other stitch, as if carrying a Fairisle colour across the back of the work. 48 sts.
Knot ends loosely so elastic does not escape; it will be adjusted at the end.
Next round: Purl.
Next round: Knit.
Rearrange sts: 18 sts on first needle; 12 sts on second; 18 sts on third needle.

Main body patt

Rounds 1, 3 and 5: (k1, skpo, k2, yf, k1) to end.
Rounds 7, 9 and 11: (k4, yf, k2tog) to end.
Even rounds: Knit.
Cont in patt for 2¾in (7cm).

At the same time work gusset as folls, working gusset incs on knit rows:
Round 4: Patt 24 sts to gusset, place marker, M2, place marker, patt 24 sts to end.
Patt as set on the 24 sts each side of gusset., and work as folls bet gusset markers:
Rounds 6 and 10: Knit.
Round 8: M1R, k2, M1L.
Round 12: M1R, k4, M1L.
Round 13: Patt across 6 gusset sts.
Round 14: M1R, k6, M1L.
Round 15: K1, patt 6, k1.
Cont in this way, inc the gusset on every knit row and knitting sts outside the central 6 st pattern within the gusset on every patt row, until there are 18 gusset sts (round 24).
Round 25: Patt across these 18 sts (the whole round is now patterned).
Cont until work measures 2¾in (7cm) (row 30 approx).
On the next knit round, knit the gusset sts, then place them on a safety pin for thumb. Cont to end of round. 48 sts.
Cont in patt until work measures 3½in (9cm) or desired length, ending with a knit row.
Next round: Purl.
Next round: M1, k to end.
Break off yarn.

Work fingers

Place all sts on waste yarn except for the first 5 sts, the last 5 sts and the M1 of the previous round. Tie the thread loosely at the little finger end. Thumb at right, work on these sts, in the round, as folls:

Little finger

Inc 3, k14.

Round 1: (k1, k2tog, k2tog, yf, k1, yf, k1) twice. 14 sts.

Round 2: Knit.

Cont until finger measures 2¼in (5.5cm).

Note: The spiral pattern is slightly different because 2 extra sts are needed for the average finger.

Next round: *(k2tog) to end.

Next round: Knit.

Break off yarn and pull end through sts to close.*

Third and second fingers

Take the next 6 sts from front and back of thread. Inc 3, k3, pick up 3 sts, k6. 18 sts.

Next round: (k2tog, k2tog, yf, k1, yf, k1) to end.

Note: If using 2 dpns, place 12 sts on the first needle and 6 sts on the second.

Work third finger to 2½in (6.5cm) and second finger to 2¾in (7cm).

Work top for both as * to *.

Forefinger (first finger)

Place last 14 sts on 2 dpns. Inc 3 at the base of second finger, k7, M1, k7. 18 sts. Work 2½in (6.5cm) in patt as for the third and second fingers, then work top as * to *.

Thumb

Place the 18 thumb sts from pin on dpns. Inc 2 sts at base of thumb.

Note: Always knit these 2 sts.

Patt as for rows 7–12 of main body patt, followed by rows 1–6 of main body pattern.

Rep these 12 rows until thumb is 2in (5cm) or desired length. Work top from * to *.

Making up

Pull gloves into shape. Darn in ends. Leave under damp cloth overnight. Adjust wrist elastic to fit and sew in ends securely.

A naked hand!

Techniques

How to make your hands decent

Measurements

Hands vary in size so gloves should always be tried on. Before begining to knit, it is a good idea to draw round the hand from the wrist, starting as close to the fingers as possible. This should allow you to measure from wrist to thumb, wrist to fingers, and the fingers.

The charts give average sizes for gloves and mittens, which are used throughout the book. Where a pattern varies from these, specific measurements will be given. Hand and finger lengths are easily varied. If you are making the gloves as a surprise, leave a spare length of yarn at the top of the fingers so they can be adjusted later if necessary.

Glove sizes

	Women	Men
Circumference	7½in (19cm)	8in (20.5cm)
Wrist to fingers	3½–3¾in (9–9.5cm)	4¼in (11cms)
Little finger	2–2⅛in (5–5.5cm)	2½in (6.5cm)
Third finger	2½in (6.5cm)	3in (7.5cm)
Second finger	2¾in (7cm)	3⅜in (8.5cm)
First finger	2½in (6.5cm)	3in (7.5cm)
Thumb	2in (5cm)	2⅛in (5.5cm)

Mitten sizes

	Ages 10–14	Women	Men
Circumference	approx. 8½in (21.5cm)	7½–7⅞in (19–20cm)	8–8¼in (20–21cm)
Length	8½in (22cm)	9in (23cm)	9¾in (25cm)
Wrist to fingers	as required	3¾in (9–9.5cm)	4¼in (11cm)

Two needles or four?

Gloves may be knitted on two needles, or using four double-pointed needles (dpns), in which case they need very little finishing.

Many four-needle designs may also be worked on two needles. Add a stitch at the beginning and end of each row for the seam. You will also need to add a seam stitch at each end of the finger rows. The simple children's glove, 'Child's play' (see page 10), gives both methods of working; you could try knitting it both ways to get the idea.

In some cases the design determines the needles; for example intarsia must be knitted on two needles over the pattern area (see 'A pride of peacocks', page 80), or the pattern yarns will always be at the wrong end for working the next row.

When worked on two needles stocking stitch is one row knit, one row purl; worked on four needles every round is worked as knit. If a pattern on four needles says '*knit* alternate rows', the same pattern for two needles would read '*purl* alternate rows'. When worked on two needles, garter stitch is every row knit; worked on four needles it is one row knit, one row purl. Unless you are an experienced knitter, do not try to change lace or slip stitch designs from 4 to 2 needles, or *vice versa*.

Whether you are knitting your gloves on 2 or 4 needles, the fingers may be worked on 2 dpns using a third to knit with. This is no more difficult than a 3-needle cast-off, and saves a lot of time when sewing up.

Tip

As a general rule, all the fingers should be started in the same place. If you are knitting for someone whose little finger is ⅜in (1cm) or more below the others, consider knitting this finger first – see 'Men's cabled gloves' (page 44).

Knitting techniques

  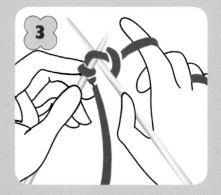

Simple cast-on

1 Form a slip knot on the left needle. Insert the right needle into the loop and wrap yarn round it as shown.

2 Pull the yarn through the first loop to create a new one.

3 Slide the loop on to the left needle. There will now be 2 sts on the left needle. Continue in this way until you have the required number of sts.

Cable cast-on

For a firmer edge, cast on the first 2 sts as shown in steps 1 and 2 (above). To cast on the third and subsequent sts, insert the needle *between* the cast-on sts on the left needle, then wrap the yarn round and pull it through to create a loop. Slide the loop on to the left needle. Repeat to end.

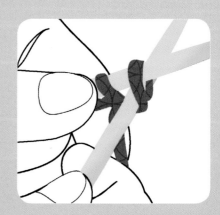

Casting off

 Knit 2 sts onto the right-hand needle. Slip the first stitch over the second (1 st on right-hand needle)

2 Knit another stitch and repeat.

Sts may also be cast off in purl: use the same technique, but purl the sts.

Rib cast-off

Work the row in rib, casting off the stitches as you go, as shown above. For example, k1, p1 rib would be worked as k1, p1 (2 sts on right-hand needle). From the right-hand needle, pass the knit stitch over the purl stitch. Knit the next stitch (2 sts on right-hand needle); pass previous purled stitch over knit stitch. Do not pull too tightly as the cast-off edge should lie flat.

Three-needle cast off

Line up 2 needles together, wrong sides facing (for a seam on the outside), or right sides facing (for a seam on the inside). For mittens the seam is usually on the outside. Arrange stitches so that there are an equal number on each needle and both needles of a pair face the same way. Using a third needle, knit together the first stitch from each needle. Repeat (2 sts on right-hand needle). Pass the first stitch over the second stitch to cast off. Repeat to end.

Variation for mittens
To make mittens symmetrical along the top, cast off the second mitten as above but purl the stitches. Adjust the tension of the cast-off so the edge lies flat.

Ⓐ Garter stitch (g-st)

On 2 needles: Knit every row.
On 4 needles: Work 1 rnd knit, 1 round purl.

Ⓑ Stocking stitch (st st)

On 2 needles: Knit on RS rows and purl on WS rows.
On 4 needles: Every round knit.

Ⓒ Shetland rib

As 2 x 2 rib but using two colours.
Cast on in colour A. Join in B.
K2A, p2B, to end. Keep stitches the same colour on subsequent rows. Take care to keep the yarn not in use at the back of the work and do not pull it too tight.

Ⓓ Single (1 x 1) rib

On 2 needles, with an even number of sts:
Row 1: *K1, p1* rep to end.
Rep for each row.

On 2 needles, with an odd number of sts:
Row 1: *K1, p1, rep from * to last st, k1.
Row 2: *P1, k1, rep from * to last st, p1.

Ⓔ Double (2 x 2) rib

On 2 needles, with an even number of sts:
Row 1: *K2, p2, rep from * to end.
Rep for each row.

Working rib on four needles

Cast on an even number of stitches and work the first row as for rib worked on two needles. On second and subsequent rows, knit each knit stitch and purl each purl stitch.

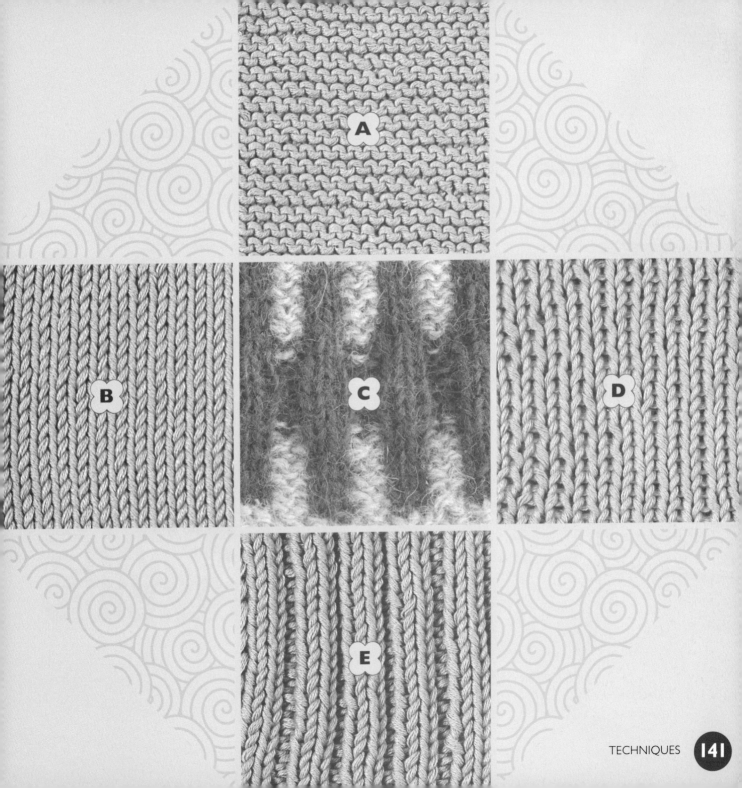

Cable stitch

These decorative stitches are quite straightforward to work, using a cable needle. Stitches are slipped on to the cable needle and knitted later to create the twists.

Front cable worked over 4 sts (cab4f)

1 Slip the next 2 sts on to a cable needle and hold in front of work.

2 Knit the next 2 stitches from the left needle as normal, then knit the 2 sts from the cable needle.

Back cable worked over 4 sts (cab4b)

Slip the next 2 sts on to a cable needle and hold at back of work.

Knit the next 2 sts from the left needle as normal, then knit the 2 sts from the cable needle.

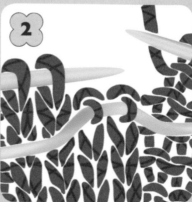

Circular knitting

1 Cast on required number of sts and divide evenly between 3 needles.

2 Lay work flat, as shown, with cast-on edge towards the centre. Working clockwise with the knit side on the outside, insert the fourth needle into the first stitch. Pick up the two needles (see illustration) in the left hand and work the stitch. Pull the yarn tight.

Note: If you find this difficult at first, work the first two rows of the pattern on two needles, then transfer them as shown. If this is stocking stitch, it should be worked 1 row purl, 1 row knit. This gives you a bit more to manipulate.

Tip

Pull the yarn tight on the second stitch of each needle to avoid creating holes.

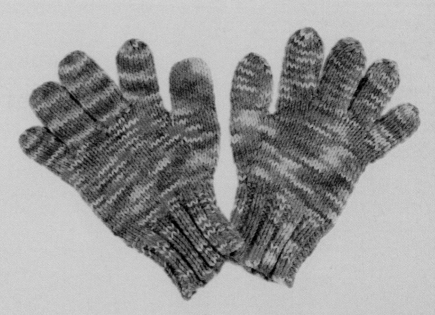

Fingers and thumbs

For gloves, a set of gusset stitches, also known as a fourchette (see instructions, right), is added between the fingers. If you are knitting on 2 needles, an extra stitch is added for the seam. Before knitting the fingers all stitches, except for those required for the first finger to be worked, are put on a thread of different coloured yarn. Stitches and fourchettes are worked according to the number given in the pattern. The first and last fingers only have a fourchette on one side.

Working the digits

 Little finger

Pick up the given number of sts from back and front on 2 needles. Working from the fourchette end, inc in first st as instructed, then knit across sts on first needle. Now, working towards the fourchette, knit sts from back needle. Join into a round and work finger on these sts using 2 or 3 needles.

 Third (ring) finger

Pick up sts from fourchette end, inc in the first st as instructed and knit across sts on the first needle. For the other fourchette, inc as required by picking up sts from the base of the previous finger. Work across sts on back needle. Join into a round and work the finger on these sts using 2 or 3 needles.

 Second finger

As for third finger.

 Forefinger (first finger)

Starting at the fourchette end, pick up sts from base of previous finger. Rotate work and knit across sts on back needle, then across sts on front needle. Join into a round and work finger on these sts on 2 or 3 needles.

 Thumb

When working on 2 needles, work the thumb as you reach it. When working on 4 needles, place the thumb stitches on a length of spare yarn and work according to the instructions given in the pattern.

 ## Fourchettes

Fourchettes are the gussets between fingers. In a normal glove, there will be a fourchette between the little finger and third finger, between the third finger and the second finger and between the second finger and the forefinger. You will need to add extra stitches to make these fourchettes. Points A to D on the left explain how this is done.

For the little finger, it is usual to cast on 2 or 3 stitches at the front. For the two middle fingers, 2 or 3 sts are added to the front and 2 or 3 are picked up from the base of the previous finger. For the forefinger, 2 or 3 sts are picked up from the base of the forefinger/second finger gap.

Fingers are knitted with the palm facing for the right hand and with the back facing for the left hand. The thumb is always to the right. If both hands are worked the same, work the fingers with the thumb to the right.

G Thumb gusset

The easiest way to work the thumb gusset is to place it in the centre (see 'Pretty in pink', page 24). You may find the fit more comfortable if the thumb gusset is moved towards the palm of the glove or mitten by about 3 sts (see 'A pride of peacocks', page 80). This means that there will be a right- and a left-hand glove.

Some mittens are made with a simple thumb, in which the stitches are cast off along the first stitches of the palm side (see 'Country garden' mittens, page 32). This is convenient if you prefer not to cut into a pattern, but it is less effective when used for the thumb of gloves, where there is more pull on the palm.

Knitting fingers on two double-pointed needle (dpns)

Avoiding holes

It is difficult to prevent holes appearing between the fingers, though these are less noticeable when they are worked in rib or if the yarn used for them is a little thicker than the yarn used for the body. Do not worry too much; they hardly show in wear and, if the yarn is wool they tend to shrink during washing.

It may help to pick up and/or cast on extra stitches for the fourchettes, then, on the second or third row. decrease to the number of stitches required. When casting on or off for the fourchettes, it may be a good idea to cast on an extra stitch, then work 2 sts together where it joins the main palm or back stitches. Another solution is to pull the stitches together from the back and add in a duplicate stitch where necessary.

1 With the third needle and the needles side by side as shown, knit along the sts on A to point B.

2 Reverse the work and continue from C to D.

3 Reverse the work and you are ready to start next round at A.

4 On the second stitch of each needle, pull the yarn hard to close up the gap from B to C and D to A.

Flip-tops

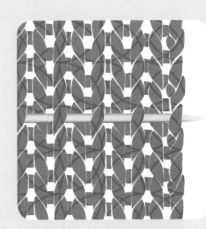

A flip-top can be added to any fingerless glove. It may also be used to add an extra layer of warmth for fully fingered gloves. Start by laying the mitten or glove on its front. Pick up the required number of stitches horizontally along the back, on the row given in the pattern, from left to right. The diagram (right) shows the stitches picked up and ready to knit. Set mitten aside.

Knitting the flip-tops

1 Cast on the same number of stitches used for the back of the mitten and work in rib for 6 or more rows to form the lapover for the front of the flip-top. Do not break off yarn. On a right side row, with the right side of the back facing, knit across both the new rib and the stitches to be picked up from the back.

2 Divide the stitches between 3 needles and join so the right sides of the work are on the outside of the circle formed. Work in the round to about 1in (2.5cm) less than the desired measurement to the top of the fingers. Place a marker at the halfway mark of the circle.

3 On the next round, k2tog tbl to dec 2 sts at the beg of the round, and k2tog to dec before the marker.

4 Repeat, working k2tog tbl to dec on the 2 sts after the marker, work to last 2 sts of round, k2tog. Cast off using the 3-needle method (see page 139).

Note: Dec on every row for children's mittens (on every other row for adult-sized mittens) until about 2–4in (5–10cm) of sts remain. Cast off.

Bell frill

This pretty trim is worked on two needles over a multiple of 14 + 4 sts, i.e. (9 + 5 = 14) sts per bell, plus 1 st at the end and 3 at the beginning. Each set of 9 sts reduces to 0, so for every (9 + 5) st bell there will be 5 sts left.

Calculating the stitches

Work out how many stitches are required for the hand and divide by 5 to produce the number of (9 + 5) bells to be worked. Add a stitch, so the first 5 sts + 1 st (6 sts) will divide into 3 sts at each end.

For the glove shown above right, the rib was worked over 56 sts. 56 sts divided by 5 = 11 + 1 stitch left over, or 11 bells (11 x 14 sts = 154 sts). The stitch left over made 155 sts, making the work symmetrical with 3 sts at each end. In this case there was no need to add an extra stitch. To work the frill on this glove, cast on 155 sts and work as sample with bracket rows repeated 10 times, not twice.

Working a sample frill

Cast on 43 sts.

Row 1: (wrong side) Work 1 row knit.

Row 2: P3 (skpo, k5, k2tog, p5) twice, reps sts inside bracket, p3 (37 sts).

Row 3: K3, (p7, k5) rep to last 10 sts, p7, k3.

Row 4: P3 (skpo, k3, k2tog, p5) twice, rep sts inside bracket, p3 (31 sts).

Row 5: K3, (p5, k5) to last 8 sts. p5, k3.

Row 6: P3, (skpo, k1, k2tog, p5) twice, rep sts inside bracket, p3 (25 sts).

Row 7: K3, (p3, k5) rep to last 6 sts, p3, k3.

Row 8: P3,(s1, k2tog, psso) twice, rep sts inside bracket, p3 (19 sts).

Row 9: P2, (p2tog, p4) to last 5 sts, p2tog, p3, (16 sts).

Note: The example was worked on a section of 3 bells, i.e. 14 x 2 sts + 11 sts. To check that your calculations are correct, you can also work backwards: 16 sts (from end of Row 9) − 1 st = 15 sts; 15 divided by 5 = 3 bells.

Colour knitting

Fairisle

Fairisle uses the stranding technique, which involves picking up and dropping yarns as they are needed. Yarns are then carried across the row and loops formed at the back of the work. These should not exceed about 5 sts in length. Make sure the tension of loops is even or the fabric may pucker.

1 Begin knitting with the first colour (A) and drop it when you need to incorporate the second (B). To pick up A again, bring it under B and knit again.

2 To pick up B again, drop A and bring B over A, then knit again.

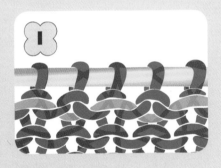

Reading charts

Most charts are shown in squares, with each square representing a stitch. They are often marked in sections of ten stitches, which makes counting easier. When working in stocking stitch on straight needles, read the chart from right to left on knit (RS) rows and from left to right on purl (WS) rows. Check carefully after every purl row to make sure the pattern stitches are in the correct place.

Intarsia

Blocks of colour are created using the intarsia technique of twisting the yarns together at the back of the work with each colour change (see diagram above). To prevent tangles, it is better to use bobbins than whole balls; they are smaller and can hang out of the way at the back of the work. Alternatively, use lengths of yarn about 2yds (2m) long, which may easily be untangled. When the work is finished, the ends are woven in at the back. Leaving to dry under a damp cloth will help to neaten any distorted stitches.

Decorative touches

Adding beads

Choose a sewing needle that will
go through the beads. Thread with
approx 6in (12.5cm) of thin cotton.
Make cotton into loop with knot.
Trim ends of loop. Insert knitting
yarn through loop. Beads should slide
down needle over knot and onto yarn.
The hole in the beads must be big
enough to take double yarn.

Note: It is a good idea to take yarn,
needle and thread along to your yarn
shop and try out beads before you buy.

1 Knit up to the stitch that is to
be beaded. Bring yarn to the front and
move the bead down close to work

2 Slip next stitch purlwise and take
yarn back ready to knit the next stitch.
The bead is held in front of the slipped
stitch as shown.

Embroidering lazy daisies

Work detached chain stitches in
a circle to form petals, as shown.
Five or six petals works best.

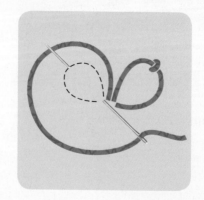

Colouring yarn

Food, household or craft dyes may be used to dye yarn, but make sure the dye you use is suitable for the yarn.

Dyeing the yarn

Wind the yarn into a single long skein. I did this by winding it round two chairs placed about 3ft (1m) apart, which produced a skein about 63in (160cms) long. Divide the skein in three along its length and tie in a figure of 8 across both sides of the skein.

Wash the yarn gently, rinse and blot off excess water with a towel. Finish as for the instructions given for your chosen dye, dipping each section into a different colour. Where the colours join you will get a mix. Experiment until you achieve the effect you want.

For the 'Dyed in the wool' mittens shown I used 'Kool-aid' dye (see right) in green, pink and blue.

'Kool-aid'

I bought my Kool-aid from the internet (www.koolaiduk.com) or you could use www.dtcrafts.co.uk, who sell it as kits, or by the packet and give a lot of information.

Making up

Seams may be joined using either mattress stitch or backstitch.

To prepare your seams for joining they should not usually be ironed. Place the gloves or mittens flat on the table with a damp cloth over them. For a flatter effect, you can also add a book (place this on a polythene bag, so the dye does not run). Leave to dry overnight.

If the seams need extra attention after joining, damp your fingers and run them along the seam. Press flat on the wrong (i.e. seam) side, using just the tip of a warm iron. Wool and cotton yarns are more robust than acrylic and artificial mixes, but take care. Heat the iron only as much as necessary to flatten the seam. If in any doubt, test the iron on your tension square first.

Mattress stitch

Thread a needle with matching yarn. Pick up two bars from one side of the work and then two from the other side. Continue along the seam in this way, pulling the seam gently together every 2–3 rows. The stitches form a ladder between the two pieces, creating a flat, secure seam.

Backstitch

Line up the two pieces of work, right sides facing, and pin together, matching patterns and rows. Insert needle and attach thread, using two small stitches. Insert needle and bring up about ¹⁄₁₆in (2mm) from start (to the left if you are right-handed). Put the needle down into the fabric at the start and bring it up about ⅛in (4mm) away. Now insert the needle back down into the left-hand hole of the last stitch and bring it up ⅛in (4mm) in front. There should be a row of stitches each ¹⁄₁₆in (2mm) long on the right side. Do not pull too tightly.

The seam should lie flat. If your yarn is textured or thicker than double knitting, split it, or use a matching finer yarn to sew the seams.

Abbreviations

approx	approximately
cont	continue
cm(s)	centimetre(s)
C	contrast
CN	cable needle
dc	double crochet
DK	double knitting
dpn(s)	double-pointed needle(s)
foll	following
g-st	garter stitch
inc	increase by working twice into the stitch
in(s)	inch(es)
K or k	knit
k-wise	with needles positioned as for a knit stitch
k2tog	knit two sts together
MC	main colour
M1	make stitch by picking up loop (see M1L and M1R)
M2	(for gusset with even number of sts.) Pick up loop as for M1 and knit into front and back of it

M1L	make 1 stitch slanting to left: pick up loop between sts from front to back with left-hand needle. Knit through back
M1R	make 1 st slanting to right: pick up loop between sts from back to front with left-hand needle. Knit into front of loop
P or p	purl
patt	pattern
p2tog	purl two stitches together
pm	place marker
psso	pass slipped stitch over
p-wise	with needles positioned as for working a purl stitch
rem	remaining
rep	repeat
RS	right side of work
skpo	slip one, knit one, pass slipped stitch over
ss	slip stitch
st(s)	stitch(es)

st st	stocking stitch (k on RS, on WS)
*	work instructions following * then repeat as directed
()	repeat instructions inside brackets as directed
WS	wrong side of work
yb	take the yarn to the back of the work (the side away from you)
yf	yarn forward: bring yarn towards you so it is at the front of the work
yo	yarn over needle
yrn	yarn round needle

Note: The last four abbreviations usually involve making an extra stitch or lace loop. However, in slip stitch and beading yf and yb mean yarn must be brought from front to back or vice versa, to make the slip stitch show the right colour or to hold the bead in place.

Conversions

Needle sizes

UK	Metric	US
14	2mm	0
13	2.5mm	1
12	2.75mm	2
11	3mm	–
10	3.25mm	3
–	3.5mm	4
9	3.75mm	5
8	4mm	6
7	4.5mm	7
6	5mm	8
5	5.5mm	9
4	6mm	10
3	6.5mm	10.5
2	7mm	10.5
1	7.5mm	11
0	8mm	11
00	9mm	13
000	10mm	15

UK/US yarn weights

UK	US
2–ply	Lace
3–ply	Fingering
4–ply	Sport
Double knitting	Light worsted
Aran	Fisherman's/worsted
Chunky	Bulky
Super chunky	Extra bulky

ABOUT THE AUTHOR

Susette has made knitwear for many years and runs knitting workshops and a helpline through her website www.susetteknits.org.uk. She knits by both hand and machine to create wonderful, workable designs that are a joy to make. Susette has wide-ranging interests: she has a BA in history and computing, an MA in Classical Civilisations from the Open University and has just completed a course in World Art and Artefacts at Birkbeck College, London, in conjunction with the British Museum.

Index

To place an order, or to request a catalogue, contact:

GMC Publications Ltd

Castle Place, 166 High Street, Lewes, East Sussex, BN7 1XU

United Kingdom

Tel: 01273 488005   **Fax:** 01273 402866

Website: www.gmcbooks.com

Orders by credit card are accepted